BACK
TO
FONT

I0110022

BACK TO FONT

Behind the Typefaces You Thought You Knew

Anitra Nottingham and Jason Phillips

CONTENTS

FOREWORD

Typefaces don't just speak for us — they speak to us. From your email signature to that report you must finish by Friday and your kid's birthday party invitation, there's a typeface for every need and every mood.

The alphabet is one of the few human tools or inventions to survive intact through tremendous technological upheaval. The history of typefaces is not just the story of the alphabet, it's a story of the alpha*better*. Designers have made (and improved) typefaces for all sorts of reasons: aesthetic and technological, certainly, but also political, philosophical and personal. Typefaces have witnessed, recorded — and occasionally even propelled — the course of human events. Their story is really *our* story, and as a species we are notoriously vain: there is nothing we find more fascinating than ourselves.

Designers have especially strong feelings about typefaces, and they use weirdly anatomical language to talk about them too. Sometimes typefaces sound like bodies, and designers like surgeons. One day we realized that this is because typefaces are kind of like people; each one has a history and a personality, and we find some attractive and some not, often for not very good reasons. Typefaces make the alphabet more than just 26 letters, they create a cast of characters experiencing the drama of ambition, rivalry, hope, frustration, fame and ignominy.

No wonder we have feelings.

Thinking about typefaces as people means we can answer all kinds of questions we never thought to ask before. Like, who were their 'parents' and 'family'? Where do they come from, and how were they 'born'? What was happening in the world at the time that influenced their growth? What's attractive and interesting about them, and what isn't? What famous person can we compare them to and why? How are typefaces used (and abused), and where can we find them 'in the wild'?

We wondered if, should we answer these questions and really get to know typefaces, would our feelings change? Would our choices? Would yours? So we started a podcast. Making *The Type Pod* revealed fascinating stories, and those stories became this book. Each chapter is like a biography of a typeface.

You can read this book in whatever order you like — end to end, or by picking the typefaces you love, hate, or have never heard of. There's probably at least one of each in here for you. Unless any of them are Helvetica and Comic Sans, because we left those out. Helvetica has its own movie, and everyone already knows that Comic Sans is terrible (except when it's perfect). Both get far too much attention already and it's time for the other typefaces, like Univers and Papyrus, to have a turn.

At the end of each chapter, we ask the same question we do at the end of our podcast. How do you really feel? Do you want to kiss, date, kill or marry this typeface?

Be warned: after reading this book you may change your default font settings (especially if you currently use Gill Sans).

Type wars

Typography (just like people) is strangely capable of starting terrible fights. Some areas of typography and type design are contested, and opinions differ. We are both graphic designers who have taught typography and graphic design history for many years. We draw on this background, and our collective years of book typesetting experience, but we don't claim to be trained historians: any mistakes are a result of this, so please keep it in mind should you decide to correct us on social media, where you can find us as @thetypepod.

Finally, there are typography terms that we will be referring to throughout the book. If you don't know these things already it will be helpful to read the introduction first — it's about type anatomy. Yes. That's a real thing.

INTRODUCTION: TYPE ANATOMY

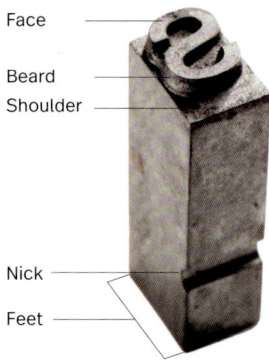

Face

Beard

Shoulder

Nick

Feet

Diagram of a metal cast sort showing its body parts.

Different parts of letters are literally named after body parts, and this is called type anatomy. Type anatomy helps designers to describe typeface characteristics, and it's the closest we get to sounding like doctors, so we like to make the most of it.

A classic graphic design student project is to make a poster of a typeface showing its anatomy. Many are like the image below, which shows you where to find the neck, shoulder, leg, arm, ear, spine, eye, foot and — of course — the crotch.

Some anatomical terms come from the time when type was physical and made of metal. The 'sort', or metal block of each individual letter, was called a body, and from this we get body copy. The space below the raised letter on a sort was a beard, the flat side the shoulder, and the whole raised part is called the face — hence typeface.

Upper and lower case

Someone had to make the sorts, and that person was the punchcutter. After the characters were designed (usually by the type designer, who got to name the typeface after themselves), technical drawings were made and transferred onto the end of a steel bar by the punchcutter.

Now the real work began. The punchcutter needed extreme skill to replicate delicate shapes and curves, carving them out of the metal using specialized tools. The insides of the letters (counterforms) were particularly tricky. Essentially they had to make the inside of the character out of a harder piece of metal and punch this counterform into the middle of the letter on the end of the original steel. This is why the insides of some letters look the same, because the punchcutters used the same tool to create the shape for multiple letters.

Folks, at this point there's just a tiny letter at the end of a metal stick. At actual size. And the work is not done. A mould would now be created by pressing the carved letter at the end of the metal stick

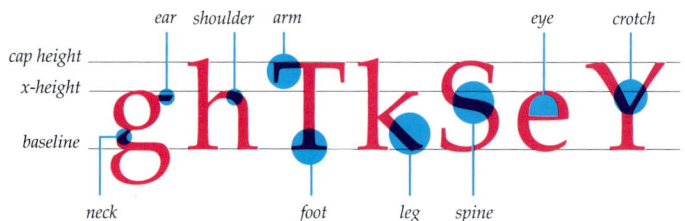

ear shoulder arm   eye   crotch

cap height

x-height

baseline

neck   foot   leg spine

Cutting a 'Q' ligature; note the scale of the fingers when compared to the size of the punch.

into a softer metal, such as copper, to create a matrix. Then an alloy of lead, antimony and tin, called 'type metal', was poured into the matrix to make the sort.

All this just to create a single piece of type — a process that had to be replicated for *every* letter at *every* size (and then the punctuation marks, and then the numbers). You can see why type designers and their punchcutters often had problematic relationships. Imagine the reaction of the poor punchcutter if after all that work Mr Big-time Type Designer announced to the studio that the letter 'C' needed to be 'a bit rounder'.

This tedious process meant that type was, for a very long time, hundreds of pieces of individual metal, some of them quite tiny. How to store such a nightmare? The answer was wooden boxes called cases. The most basic sorting method was to separate the capitals from the not-capitals, storing capitals in the case above the work bench and not-capitals in the one below the workbench: hence they would be referred to as 'upper case' and 'lower case'.

Each typeface would be stored in separate cases, of course. You can now see why metal characters were called 'sorts', because someone had to sort them in order to store them. (That someone was the apprentice, also called a 'printer's devil', but more on that later.)

Who knows if cramming all those sorts into small wooden boxes made the printers start thinking of them as families. But they did, and at some point the idea stuck, so now typefaces come in 'families'.

Which makes them sound even more like people, and brings us to why you should *not* call typefaces 'fonts'.

The punch (left) and the matrix created from the punch (right).

A typesetter's tools c.1740, including the cases holding the sorts.

Call them typefaces

Most people, even lots of graphic designers, call typefaces 'fonts'. We bowed to the inevitable and named this book *Back to Font*, although technically it should be called *Back to Typeface*.

To be precise, a 'font' is a style of a typeface, and a bunch of fonts of the same typeface collected together is a font family. Most typefaces come with standard fonts such as bold, roman and italic. Some typefaces have fonts with names like Great Primer, Double Pica Roman Capitals, Brevier Number 1 Roman, or Two-line Double Pica Italic Caps because they are a fancy family who like to sound like an artisanal coffee order.

Looking at you, Baskerville.

Although 'font' works better in the title, we still feel a bit bad about not trying harder to use 'typeface'. Using 'font' is blatant pandering, and we do know better. Sorry, designers.

Serif and sans serif

It's often said that there are two types of people in the world, but there are actually two kinds of typefaces in the world: serif and sans serif.

A serif is the short line that crosses the top and bottom of the strokes in a letterform. There are multiple kinds of serifs, including hairline, bracketed, slab, wedge and glyphic. Typefaces without a serif are called 'sans serif' — 'sans' means 'without'.

serifs *(Times New Roman)*

hairline serifs *(Bodoni)*   bracketed serifs *(Baskerville)*   slab serifs *(Rockwell)*   wedge serifs *(Wide Latin)*   glyphic serifs *(Trajan)*

sans serifs *(Futura)*

Of course, it's not quite that simple. Some typefaces bulge at the ends and look like they want to have a serif but don't, like Optima. Others have very tiny serifs that are barely noticeable, like Copperplate.

To make things even more confusing, script typefaces — which look like calligraphy — don't fit into either category.

There are many arguments had about whether serif or sans serif is more readable, and in which context. These arguments are fun, and we have some of them in this book.

Wooden type was cheap and, according to the fine printers of the time, nasty.

Display typefaces

Some typefaces are meant for greater things than body copy. These are called display typefaces. The origins of display, or title faces, lie in those illuminated letters from medieval manuscripts — what we now know as drop cap(ital)s. These big letters were meant to be arresting, intriguing and unique; quite a different aesthetic from body text, which is governed by conformity, uniformity and repetition.

18th-century printers used sand and wooden patterns to cast large letterforms for poster and signage printing, because the larger the punch, the more difficult it was to create the matrix evenly.

In around 1810 William Caslon IV, a member of a printing/type design dynasty, introduced a new type of matrix he called sanspareil (or 'unmatched'). He cut sheet metal into the shape of the letter then riveted this to a backing plate prior to casting the final metal sort.

The prevalence of posters and commercial signage throughout the 19th century encouraged the development of new styles of typefaces to attract attention, such as bold stroke weights, exaggerated serifs and even extremely condensed fonts.

Linotype machines were used for a surprisingly long time. Here are some typesetters at work in 1935. *The New York Times* only decommissioned their machines in 1971.

Then, in the 1880s, Linotype was invented. This involved machinery that could literally cast a 'line-o'-type' in hot metal, which could be re-melted and used again and again. Instead of setting each individual letter by hand, type could now be set quickly, anywhere (where you could fit a large machine) and on-demand. In a way that's very familiar to us now, this disruptive technology sent the US printing industry into something of a crisis towards the end of the century as the demand for handset body type plummeted.

In 1892, 23 of the then 34 US type companies, called foundries, amalgamated to form the American Type Founders Company. Two years later, the new general manager, Robert Wickham Nelson, cannily recognized that as body type was being replaced by Linotype, display type would now be the business mainstay of the mega-foundry. This was a pivot from producing masses of small metal type for hand-setting to producing larger, more unique display typefaces for headings, because display type was still easier to set by hand than to cast in hot metal over and over.

True purpose-built display typefaces have no lowercase letters because they were made to be used for headlines and at larger sizes. Other typefaces effectively function as display typefaces because, although they have lowercase letters, they cannot be read well at body copy sizes.

A true display typeface such as Copperplate can be used for lots of purposes. Like a vanilla sponge it has little 'flavour' and is capable of soaking up different meanings. Other display typefaces have very distinctive 'flavours' and are more like fish sauce: intense, and best used only in certain kinds of dishes. (Or to create an interesting contrast with the subject matter, like fish-sauce ice cream.)

Script typefaces can be used as display typefaces or as body copy, but they must be set so that the letters join up. To do otherwise is to commit a type crime.

Italics

Nowadays, an italic font is a standard variant for almost all typefaces, and we use italics for stress — the typographic equivalent of an underline — or to distinguish one part of the text from the main passage, such as a quote, or to indicate the title of a publication or film.

Originally, Italic was a distinct typeface. Until the late 15th century the dominant style of penmanship was Chancery hand, a version of Blackletter, which the historian, poet and early humanist Francis Petrarch brutally dissed as having been 'designed for something other than reading'.

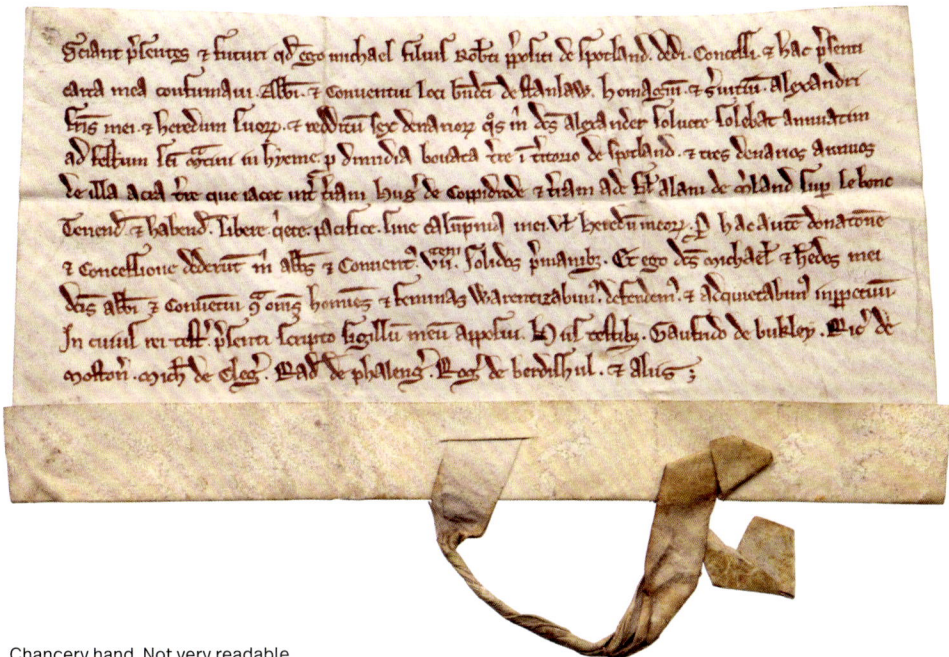

Chancery hand. Not very readable.

ALDVS STVDIOSIS
OMNIBVS.   S.

P. V · M · Bucolica · Georgica · Aeneida quam emenda
ta, et qua forma damus, uidetis, cætera, quæ Poeta
exercēdi sui gratia composuit, et obscœna, quæ ei
dem adscribuntur, nō cēsuimus digna enchiridio.
E st animus dare posthac ijsdem formulis optimos
quosque autores .   Valete.

IN GRAMMATOGLYPTAE
LAVDEM.

Qui graijs dedit Aldus, en latinis
D at nunc grammata sculpta dædaleis
F rancsci manibus Bononiensis .

MVSEVM
BRITANNICVM

P · V · M · MANTVANI BV
COLICORVM
TITYRVS .

Melibœus · Tityrus .

T ityre tu patulæ recubās sub tegmi
ne fagi   Me.
Syluestrem tenui musam meditæ
ris auena .
Nos patriæ fines, et dulcia linqui
mus arua .
N os patriam fugimus, tu Tityre lentus in mbra
F ormosam resonare doces Amaryllida syluas .
O Melibœe, deus nobis hæc ocia fecit .   Ti.
N anq; erit ille mihi semper deus illius aram
S æpe tener nostris ab ouilibus imbuet agnus .
I lle meas errare boues, ut cernis, et ipsum
L udere, quæ uellem, cælamo permisit agresti .
N on equidem inuideo, miror magis. undiq; totis Me.
V sque adeo turbatur agris. en ipse capellas
P rotinus æger ago. hanc etiam uix Tityre duco .
H ic inter densas corylos modo nanq; gemellos .
S pem gregis, ah silice in nuda connixa reliquit .
S æpe malum hoc nobis, si mens non leua fuisset,
D e cœlo tactas memini prædicere quercus .
S æpe sinistra caua prædixit ab ilice cornix .
S ed tamen, iste deus qui sit, da Tityre nobis .
V rbem, quam dicunt Romam, Melibœe putaui Ti.
S tulius ego huic nostræ similem· quo sæpe solemus

Page from Aldus Manutius's 1501
edition of the Aldine Virgil, featuring
the first italic typeface.

Aldus Manutius, a Venetian printer, released the first complete volume to use what we now know as italics in a 1501 edition of Virgil's poetry. By replicating the trend of cursive handwriting of the period, instead of the more rigid, traditional Chancery hand, he hoped to give his books a hip appeal.

Palaeographer James Wardrop, in his analyses of writing systems, has suggested the hallmark of Italic was its utility; an informality that improved the speed of both reading and writing.

To more closely resemble handwriting, Aldus Manutius's edition of Virgil featured at least 65 ligatures. These are characters that combine two letters into one neat and eye-pleasing form which otherwise, when set side by side, might tangle with each other. Think of the teardrop terminal of an 'f' next to the dot of an 'i'. This many special characters created a tremendous amount of work for Manutius's punchcutter, Francesco Griffo, and probably contributed to the two falling out shortly afterwards.

Aldus Manutius started a trend for small, easily portable editions of popular books, often collections of poems, called octavos. Each line of poetry in the volume began with an upright roman capital, with a distinct space before the first lowercase letter of the rest of the line set in italic.

Italics really took off. Increased book sales, with more words to the page — *ker ching* — meant that everyone wanted in on the action. In the grand tradition of type design, other printers turned to plagiarism.

Manutius attempted to stem the tide of piracy by issuing the early equivalent of product warning labels:

> *It happens that in the city of Lyon our books appeared under my name, but full of errors… and deceived unwary buyers due to the similarity of typography and format… Furthermore, the paper is of poor quality and has a heavy odour…*

Unfortunately, the detailed descriptions he included of those errors allowed the fakers to improve their product and make the piracy harder to detect. By 1512 the design had spread as far as Paris, and the new style of lettering was now referred to as 'italics', from its country of origin — Italy.

The Vox-ATypl classification system

If you want to talk about (or sell) a group of similar things it helps to organize them into groups or classes. The Vox-Atypl classification system (Vox system) categorizes typefaces based on shared characteristics, the same way botany and zoology systems arrange similar plants and animals within species and families. We use the Vox system in this book because (for better or worse) people get sorted into categories too.

The system was created in 1954 by Maximilien Vox, an art theorist and historian of French typography, and its creation is a whole story in itself (see the *Novarese* chapter).

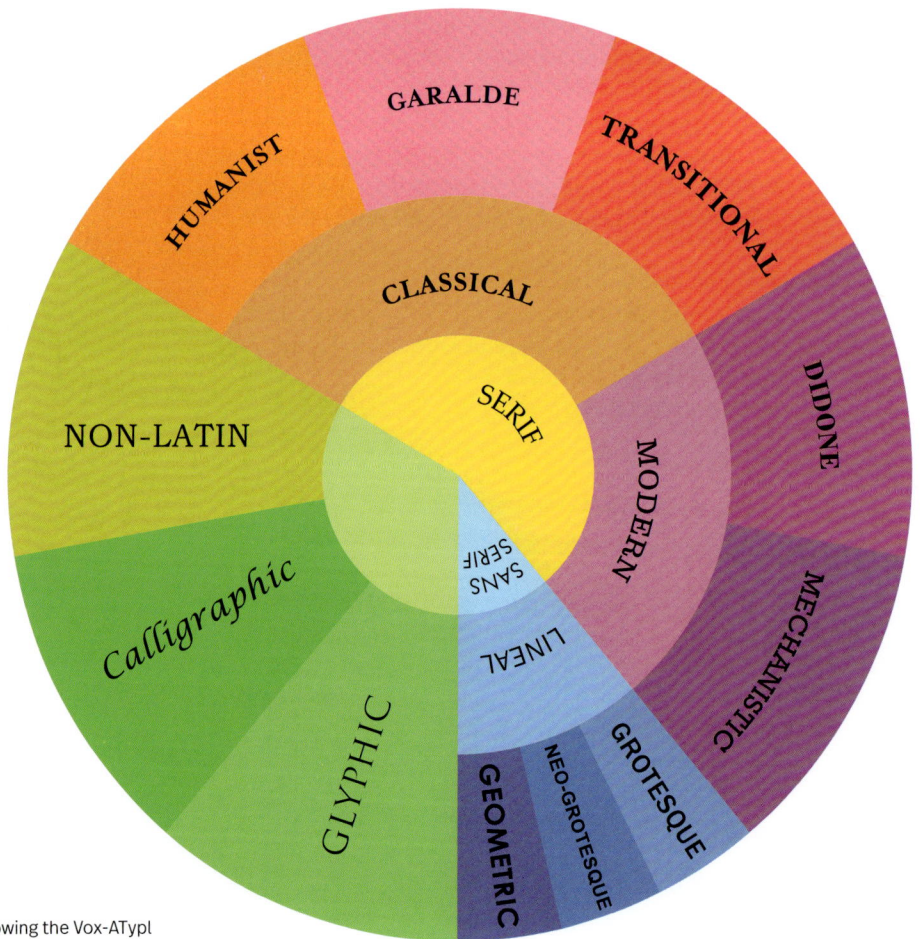

Diagram showing the Vox-ATypl classification system.

The international typography body (yes, there is such a thing), called Association Typographique Internationale (ATypI), adopted the Vox system in 1962 and it became a British Standard in 1967.

The Vox system divides typefaces into classes, categories and subcategories by criteria based on their main characteristics. We will explain more about these characteristics in the individual chapters.

Classicals includes the subcategories *Humanist*, *Garalde* and *Transitional*.

Moderns includes the subcategories *Didone*, *Mechanistic* and *Lineal*. 'Lineal' means 'sans serif' and is further divided into the subcategories of *Grotesque*, *Neo-grotesque* and *Geometric*.

By the way, *Didone* is a celebrity portmanteau of the surnames of two famous type designers, Firmin Didot and Giovanni Bodoni. *Garalde* comes from two other famous type designers, Claude Garamond and Aldus Manutius (Aldus Manutius fans call Garaldes *Aldines* — because of course they do).

Calligraphic is made up of the categories: *Glyphic*, *Script*, *Graphic*, *Blackletter* and, the most recently added, *Gaelic*.

Non-Latin *Latin* is the term for the letters used in European writing systems, so all other typefaces from other writing systems (such as Greek, Cyrillic, Hebrew, Arabic, Chinese and Korean) are grouped together and defined by what they are not. Rude. But better than the previous term: *Exotics*.

In 2021 ATypI decided to 'de-adopt' the Vox system and set up a working group to come up with a new system that would be truly international and include the non-Latin typefaces. An incredibly difficult task, so that's probably why there's still nothing more than an announcement on the ATypI website at the time of this book going to press. Even a temporary page housing the extensive working group code of conduct has been taken down.

That an extensive code of conduct was needed in the first place gives you a clue as to just how strong feelings about typography can get.

So, there you have it: type anatomy isn't just a quirky way to name the bits and pieces of letters; it's a testament to the painstaking craft and rich history behind every typeface. But if you think the drama ends here, hold on to your serifs and keep reading.

Times New Roman

Designer: Stanley Morison
Date: 1932

A serious Stanley Morison.

For graphic designers, Times New Roman is not a design option, it's merely a typeface used in Word documents that are then sent to us to turn into something more interesting. You probably used Times New Roman for your school assignments. Maybe it's your email typeface, and you doubtless use it at work. Times New Roman is a default: invisible and bereft of personality. We didn't even use Times New Roman to draft this book, we chose Cambria so as not to bore Roger, the book's designer.

You might be wondering why we made Times New Roman the first chapter. It's not so we could talk about hot metal typesetting (although it's not *not* because of that). Times New Roman is here at the beginning because we can thank — or blame — the typographer, printing historian and all-round giant of typography Stanley Morison for Times New Roman. Morison was famously uncompromising and fierce about typographic quality. We think of him as the kind of art director who would send back every piece of work with a note attached saying, 'I have thoughts, we need to talk'.

You probably haven't heard about Stanley, but we think you should, because he's great — even if Times New Roman isn't.

Mr Stanley 'I have thoughts' Morison

Stanley Morison was born in 1889 in Wanstead, back then a borough of Essex, on the outskirts of London in the UK. His father walked out on the family when he was still a child, and young Stanley had to go to work right after primary school to help his family eat. But he didn't let this misfortune hold him back. While working as a clerk from 1905 — 1912, he educated himself at the local library. It worked: the editor of *The Times* newspaper would later call him 'the most intelligent man in Europe'.

abcdefghijklm
nopqrstuvwxyz
ABCDEFGHIJKLM
NOPQRSTUVWXYZ
0123456789!?

abcdefghijklm
nopqrstuvwxyz
ABCDEFGHIJKLM
NOPQRSTUVWXYZ
0123456789!?

THE ⟨crest⟩ TIMES

NEW TYPE

on and after

MONDAY OCTOBER 3

On Monday, October 3, THE TIMES will appear printed throughout in a new type specially designed for easy reading. The change will be made with the approval of the most eminent medical opinion. The type which is now displaced has long been a model for newspapers throughout the world, but, in response to the need, under modern conditions, of relieving the eye of all possible strain, a new standard of clearness and legibility will be set up.

On Monday also THE TIMES returns to an older and simpler form for its main heading. The Gothic title which, a little more than 100 years ago, supplanted the original Roman heading of THE TIMES and became, accidentally, the commonplace heading for all newspapers, has been dropped. The straightforward style, now reinstated, is typical of the great gain in clearness of print which has been achieved on every page. The simplicity of the whole title-piece has been served by the re-establishment of the Royal coat of arms as THE TIMES presented it in the last decade of the eighteenth century. It is reproduced at the beginning of this announcement. To its many distinctive features THE TIMES thus adds its heading. It is as a heading should be, immediately recognizable, and it is free from affectation, in accordance with tradition, and typographically consistent.

The new letterpress is the result of years of research and experiment by THE TIMES. For the first time a newspaper has designed its own printing type. It meets the difficulties of reading in trains and cars and by artificial light.

"PRINTING THE TIMES"	"READING THE TIMES"
THE NEW TYPE AND HEADING ARE DESCRIBED, AND THE REASONS FOR THE CHANGE EXPLAINED, IN A SPECIALLY WRITTEN BOOKLET ENTITLED "PRINTING THE TIMES."	AN ILLUSTRATED BOOKLET WHICH IS A GUIDE TO THE CONTENTS AND MAKE-UP OF THE PAPER FOR THOSE WHO ARE NOT YET REGULAR READERS.

THESE TWO BOOKLETS MAY BE HAD FREE AND POST FREE ON APPLICATION TO THE PUBLISHER, THE TIMES, PRINTING HOUSE SQUARE, E.C.4, OR THROUGH NEWSAGENTS AND BOOKSTALLS.

THE TIMES—EASIEST TO READ AND BEST WORTH READING

The issues of The Times Weekly Edition, The Times Literary Supplement, The Times Educational Supplement, and The Times Trade and Engineering Supplement will appear in the new Roman type during and after the week ending October 8.

Front page of *The Times* from September 1932, announcing the imminent change of typeface to Times New Roman.

The Times both inspired Morison's life's work and was responsible for his most famous work. His interest in typography and type design was sparked by an article about printing in *The Imprint*, a supplement of the newspaper. He answered an ad in the supplement and secured a job there as an assistant in 1913 (it sure sounds easier for a man without a formal education to get a job back then).

Morison would go on to work as a design director for various publishers, including Burns & Oates, Pelican Press and Cloister Press. In 1923 he was made typographic advisor (a job title we covet) for the British Monotype Corporation, where he commissioned the famous typeface Gill Sans from a young Eric Gill in 1927. Some of Morison's other famous commissions while at Monotype were Bembo, Ehrhardt, Bell and Perpetua.

Stanley Morison is part of the storied typographic history of Cambridge University, serving as its typographic advisor from 1923 to 1959. He was a staff editor and writer for the graphic arts journal *The Penrose Annual* from 1925 to 1930, and worked for *The Times* from 1933 to 1967, becoming editor of the *Times Literary Supplement* after World War II when post-war austerity meant typographic work was scarce. And it's only in the last line of his glowing biography entry that the *Encyclopedia Britannica* coyly mentions that he was on this famous reference work's board of editors.

Morison made a living by having strong views on type, and he had other strong views, too. After converting to Catholicism aged 19, he only ever wore black suits from an ecclesiastical outfitter. A friend once claimed Morison wore his hat one size too small, perhaps having decided that his head was smaller than it actually was. Whatever the reason, it's a strong fashion statement. Morison also held fierce political views. He was a Marxist and a pacifist, and was jailed for being a conscientious objector during World War I. This showed great strength of character, as the pressure to conform at that time was immense. Later in life, Morison turned down both a knighthood and a CBE.

Fleuron and other dingbats

Morison was a founding member of the Fleuron Society, which sounds like a shadowy cabal but was just a group of type nerds. He edited their beautifully typeset journal of typography *The Fleuron* from 1926 to 1930. A 'fleuron' is the technical term for a floral ornament, like those used in the typeface Zapf Dingbats. Morrison had thought *The Fleuron* hit the right notes of history and romance to appeal to non-type-nerd people, but this sadly didn't result in huge sales. There were only 1,370 copies ever made, and they are still surprisingly affordable at antique book dealers if you want to buy one.

You might be lucky enough to find copies of *The Fleuron* in your state library collection, like we did. It's worth arranging to look at them in person, as they are lovely examples of fine typography.

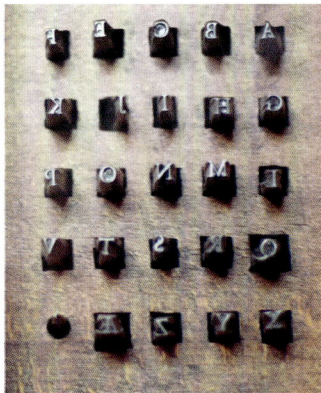

What's left of the original Plantin typeface.

Morison had a storied 'portfolio' career, with a lot of roles on the go at once. He was not a type designer, but rather a typographer steeped in fine typography of the most classic kind. The designer and friend of Morison Beatrice Warde once called this 'crystal goblet' typography, designed to be self-effacing, to disappear so that only the words would be noticed; the kind of typography that postmodernist designers like David Carson would totally reject in the 1990s.

Sloppy typographic discipline

Morison designed Times New Roman as a 'new roman' typeface for *The Times* partly to get more type onto a page and save paper costs, but also because he (like all typographers) was fussy. In a classic example of Morison 'having thoughts', he complained that the newspaper's existing typeface was inadequate and had a 'sloppy sense of typographic discipline'. It's not entirely clear what this means, but by this point in his career Morison was so respected that he could just say something like this, and *The Times* would respond with, 'Yes! We see the lack of typographic discipline, let's change that!'

Times New Roman is not 'new', it is a revival of Plantin, a typeface designed in the 16th century by Antwerp printer Christophe Plantin. A 'revival' is a remake of a typeface. Originally typefaces were made by one print shop, and the sorts (metal pieces) could be easily lost or destroyed. If you wanted a typeface you would have to redraw it from printed specimens and cut a new version out of metal. To this day a version of a typeface is still called a 'cut'.

Making a revival is not considered plagiarism. Often there are very good reasons to make a new cut of a typeface, perhaps because the original is lost, or to optimize it for new technology. Sometimes the typeface will be considerably altered in the process to create something new, which was the case with Times New Roman, when in the late 20th century new cuts were made to create digital typefaces.

Morison was the design lead for Times New Roman. The person who did the actual work of drawing the letterforms was a *Times* employee called Victor Lardent. He was chosen because he could do a 'lean and hard line' — which is just one of many design-related sayings that sound a bit rude out of context.

Morison was so involved with the design of Times New Roman that he considered this his only typeface design, and we are not going to argue with him.

An advertisement for a Linotype machine in 1888.

(below) A still from a film about the very last day the linotype machines were used at *The New York Times* in 1978.

Hot metal typesetting

At Monotype, Stanley Morison commissioned cuts of classic typefaces optimized for hot metal Linotype machines, which made setting type by hand much faster. A typesetter typed in 90 characters — about a line, hence 'line-o'-type' — into the machine.

The Linotype machine would cast that line, called a 'slug', out of a blob of hot metal. Multiple slugs and handset headlines were then arranged by hand into a form, knocked down with hammers and locked

MEMORANDUM

ON A PROPOSAL TO REVISE

THE TYPOGRAPHY OF

The Times

1930

Morison wrote an exhaustive 34-page memo to convince *The Times* committee, which schooled its members in typography and included a line that showed he knew he was laying it on a bit thick: 'But more (alas for the committee!) of this later.'

in to make a page. The page was then cast into a curved lead plate for printing. Once printed, slugs were melted down and used again. The impurities that rose to the surface during this process were called 'dross', which became an insulting term for many things, including bad writing.

Linotype machines were used for a hundred years, and the company that made them still exists today. It's very likely you have Monotype's cut of Times New Roman, which was one of the first digital cuts and comes pre-loaded on computers. Times New Roman has always been a machine-age creation, even if it was first made for machines that used hot metal instead of pixels.

Controversy

Times New Roman wasn't designed to create an identity for the newspaper like typefaces are today. It was just designed to be readable, work with the technology and save space. The first time the typeface was used in the paper was October 3rd, 1932, and it only received one letter of complaint. Probably because it did its job and disappeared, or maybe because they did not have social media back then.

In 1994 the typographer Mike Parker showed that Times New Roman was also based on a typeface designed in 1904 by the rather dazzlingly named Starling Burgess. But it wasn't until 2007 that *The Times* added this to their official history of Times New Roman (*The Times* is probably lucky that social media wasn't around in 1994).

Now we have laid out his bonafides we feel bad about saying this, but Times New Roman is not Stanley's best work — and he seems to have realized it. In his 'typographic memoir' *A Tally of Types* (and can we just say, what a jolly-good-chaps-tally-ho-tea-and-crumpets title that is?) he wrote an imaginary quote about it in the manner of art critic and famous wallpaper designer William Morris:

> As a new face it should, by the grace of God and the art of man, have been broad and open, generous and ample; instead, by the vice of Mammon and the misery of the machine, it is bigoted and narrow, mean and puritan.

This 'quote' brilliantly captures exactly what we think William Morris must have been like: insufferable, which is just one reason Stanley Morison is on the list of people invited to our imaginary historical dinner party and William Morris is not.

Times New Roman, the ideal workhorse

Times New Roman is a serif typeface that falls under 'Transitional' in the Vox type classification system. Meaning it's modern but retains traces of the humanist typefaces that came before it and were modelled on handwriting.

Times New Roman's biggest sin visually is that it's narrow and contrasty, but it's otherwise, you know, fine. The bold font is very bold, which works well at small sizes in a newspaper but makes the subheadings on your school essays look bad.

Also, the italic is terrible. Just look at it.

Morison believed italics shouldn't exist, so perhaps that's the reason, but another theory is that this is because they are wider — the same horizontal width as the roman. A design choice that would make it easier to calculate 'copy fit', or how much type would fit on a page. If there wasn't enough space the writers had to cut text. Writers hate that.

Copy-fitting maths was hideous. You had to calculate characters per pica — which varied between typefaces — then use a formula to check that the column width and length would allow enough space, and… well, everything is just much easier to do on a computer, isn't it?

Apart from these quibbles, Times New Roman gets the job done and doesn't get in the way. Which is what Morison wanted, so good job there, Stanley.

Lorem ipsum

Lorem ipsum

Lorem ipsum

Times New Roman in roman, bold and italic

M B run

Times New Roman's roman compared to italics

Times New Roman in the wild

Before Times New Roman came pre-loaded on every computer and thus became a default choice, designers would use it more intentionally, based on its own merits. Perhaps for this reason you will find Times New Roman on a surprising number of classic album and vintage book covers, as it works across multiple genres.

One example of using Times New Roman for a high-profile design is the logo of the *Star Wars* movie *Return of the Jedi*. It's used for the 'return of the Jedi' bit (the *Star Wars* bit is called Star Jedi, and that was designed by Suzy Rice under instructions from George Lucas to make the type look a 'bit fascist').

You may already use Times New Roman as your default typeface, but should you?

Kiss, date, marry or kill?

We do appreciate Stanley Morison, and also the intention behind Times New Roman, but we choose to kill. Or more accurately, ignore. Because, as a default, it effectively doesn't exist. We are way too concerned about what other people might think of us if we actually designed something with it, so we never have.

Times New Roman, personality-wise, is a bit like Hugh Grant in *Four Weddings and a Funeral*: self-effacing, and so terribly wet compared to the other quirky characters. Do we even know what Hugh does when he's not at weddings and funerals? Do we care? No. Times New Roman is the same: just not as interesting as the other typefaces. As Vincent Connare, the designer of Comic Sans, once said, this is what makes Times New Roman a worse choice than Comic Sans.

He's right. At least you know where you stand with Comic Sans.

(above) Times New Roman evokes a certain gravitas, whether you're the Australian Government or a small independent college.

(right) Luxury fragrance Lanvin uses an extended version of Times New Roman on its packaging.

(opposite) A rare sighting of the typeface in something interesting: the poster for *Star Wars: Return of the Jedi*.

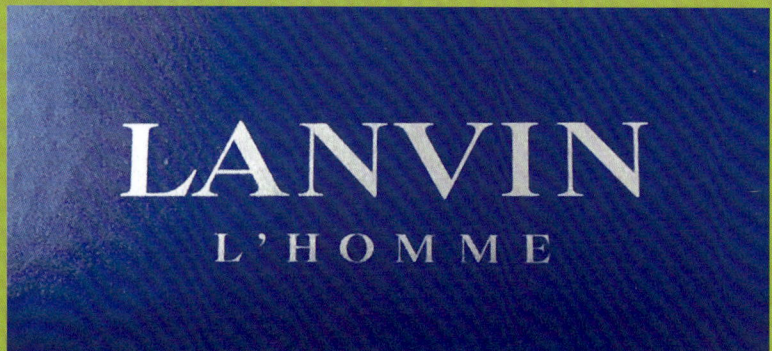

Gill Sans

Designer: Eric Gill
Date: 1928

Eric Gill wearing what appears to be a box on his head – and this is not even his weirdest look.

In the mid-2000s the Folio Society released a magnificent (and quite expensive) limited-edition facsimile of Eric Gill's *The Four Gospels*. It looks very impressive on a bookshelf. Unfortunately, our appreciation for this objectively beautiful example of the typographer's art has been tainted by revelations about Gill's personal life.

It can be difficult, even actively painful, to separate the art from the artist — especially for those of us who forked out a lot of money for *The Four Gospels*. So in this chapter we will not even attempt to do so, we are just going to feel the feelings.

Now, it's not often (ever?) that a book about typography needs a content warning, but this one does. Some of this chapter could be triggering for anyone who has experienced abuse, so we will let you know when to skip ahead if you need to.

Eric Gill: not a member of Monty Python

Gill Sans was the first typeface to be designed by Eric Gill — who sounds a bit like an early member of the surreal comedy troupe Monty Python, dropped from the line-up before they hit the big time. Gill was an artist, sculptor and letter-cutter with a sideline in erotic woodcuts. He was a well-known and accomplished illustrator of both the sacred and the profane (and on the profane side we include those erotic woodcuts), and a typeface designer.

Eric was born Arthur Eric Rowton Gill (so you can understand why he might have gone with the punchier 'Eric') in Brighton, UK, in 1882. His father was a priest, and many of his brothers and sisters became missionaries or nuns. Gill attended the Chichester School of Art and was then apprenticed to an ecclesiastical architect, William Douglas Caröe. An ecclesiastical architect was a thing back then; nowadays, you'd probably cop some odd looks if you introduced yourself that way at parties.

abcdefghijklm
nopqrstuvwxyz
ABCDEFGHIJKLM
NOPQRSTUVWXYZ
0123456789!?

abcdefghijklm
nopqrstuvwxyz
ABCDEFGHIJKLM
NOPQRSTUVWXYZ
0123456789!?

ABCDEFGH
IJKLMNQRS
TUWXYZ

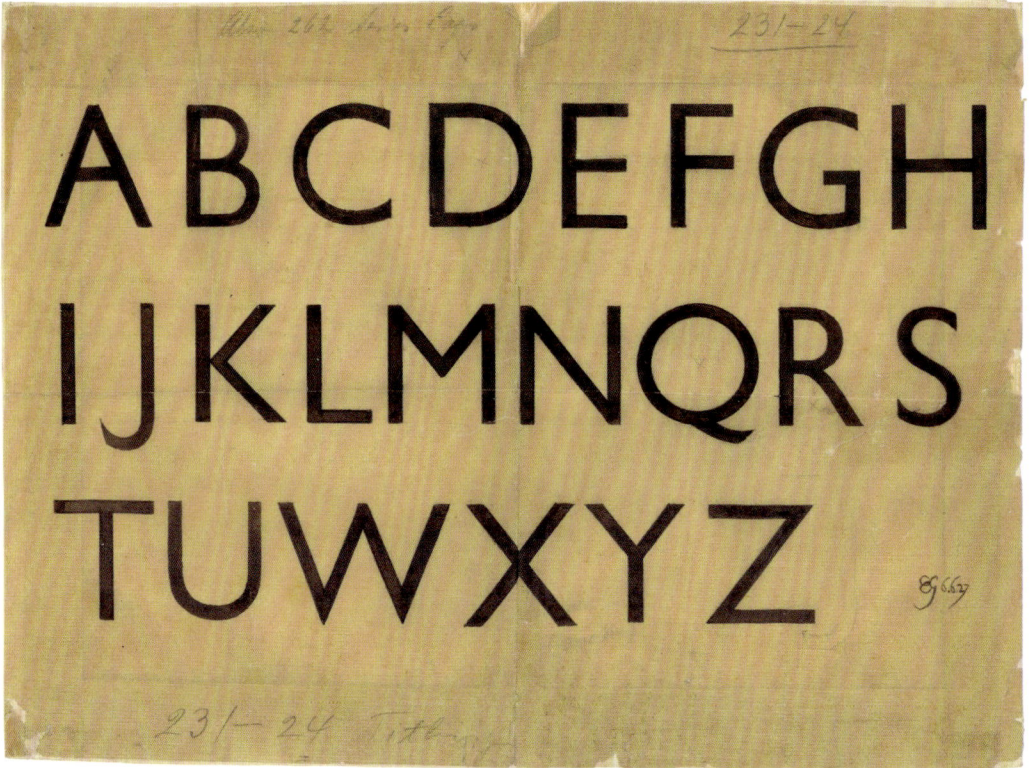

(above) Some original drawings for the Monotype face signed by Eric Gill, 1927.

(right) The interior of St Peter's church, Gorleston-on-Sea.

Gill Sans

The sculpture of Prospero and Ariel at BBC HQ, which depicts the air spirit (perhaps tellingly) as a naked child. This photo was taken before the sculpture was damaged by a protester, who had spent four hours hitting it on the leg with a hammer.

There is only one example of Gill's church architecture, the beautifully spare St Peter's, located in the delightfully British-sounding Gorleston-on-Sea on the English coast. Gill studied stone-cutting at Westminster. As a sculptor he worked on some large commissions, including the *Stations of the Cross* at Westminster Cathedral and several war memorials (interesting work, given that he was an avowed pacifist). Perhaps his best-known sculptural work is of Prospero and Ariel from Shakespeare's *The Tempest*, which stands above the entrance of the BBC headquarters in London.

While still working as an architect, Gill took night classes at London's Central School of Arts and Crafts. He studied with Edward Johnston, designer of the London Underground typeface, who taught calligraphy there. This was where Gill's typographic journey began: he started a side hustle, and by 1906 his tombstone carving, calligraphy and lettering business had grown so much that he could quit his day job and start his own studio.

One of Gill's *Stations of the Cross* sculptures at Westminster Cathedral in London.

VENIT HORA UT CLARIFICETUR FILIUS HO— MINIS

AMEN·AMEN
DICO·VOBIS
NISI· GRA-
NUM· FRU-
MENTI·CAD-
ENS·IN·TER-
kAM·MORTU-
UM·FUERIT
IPSUM·SOLU
MANET·SI
AUTEM
MORTUU
FUERIT
MULTUM
FRUCTUM
AFFERT

QVI·AMAT·ANIMAM·SUAM
PERDET·EAM·ET·QVI·ODIT
ANIMAM·SUAM·IN·HOC
MUNDO·IN·VITAM·AETER-
NAM·CUSTODIT·EAM

XIV THE BODY OF JESUS IS LAID IN THE TOMB

In 1927 Stanley Morison of the Monotype Corporation was impressed by a sign for a Bristol bookseller that Gill had hand-painted, and invited him to design his first typeface, which became Gill Sans. Gill went on to design more typefaces, including the classics Perpetua and Joanna.

Gill was made an Honorary Associate of the Institute of British Architects in 1935 and given their highest accolade, Royal Designer for Industry, in 1936. This is like the Order of the Garter for British designers (but with 200 members at any given time instead of 24). In 1937 he was made an Associate of the Royal Academy, and over the years he wrote around 300 essays on art and religion. Gill died at home after an operation to treat lung cancer in 1940 (which, if you have seen the first episode of the Netflix show *The Crown*, you'll know was an even more terrible way to go back then than it is today).

Now, this all sounds respectable, right? But here is your first content warning.

If you don't wish to read about abuse, skip to 'A modern typeface for a turbulent time'

It turns out that Gill had kept diaries that detailed not only numerous extramarital affairs with the family's servants (and others), but also a long incestuous relationship with his sister, Gladys.

Disturbingly, he also wrote in detail about abusing his own young daughters, Betty and Petra. Petra insisted until the end of her life that she wasn't abused. We respect her right to say so, but undoubtedly what happened fits the definition of abuse. As Petra herself has said in interviews, she didn't go to school, so she didn't know what was 'normal'. To top it all off Eric also had, shall we say, an unhealthy interest in the family dog.

This all remained secret until Fiona MacCarthy's 1989 biography of Gill, which started the decline of his reputation. Calls to boycott Eric Gill gathered momentum after the #metoo movement in 2014, and in 2022 the famous British auction house Christie's announced it would no longer handle Gill's work. One of his war memorials has been removed, there are calls for the *Stations of the Cross* to be moved from Westminster Cathedral, and someone attacked the statue of Prospero and Ariel at the BBC with a hammer: honestly, we can understand the outrage.

What was the trouble with Gill?

Gill was, let's just say, a very *intense* Christian. He and his wife Ethel converted to Catholicism in 1913. He was one of the founding members of an artistic community in Ditchling, Sussex, which he left in 1924 when the group wanted to open up to the village community: too much of a secular modern world for Eric. He didn't believe in indoor plumbing or ovens, and banned typewriters from his house. When Gill moved his family to a derelict abbey in Wales called Capel-y-ffin he effectively created a cult centred around himself, and took to wearing a habit with a rope belt, symbolic of chastity (ironic much?).

By this stage Gill rocked an Amish-style beard and a wide-eyed look. We've all seen enough pseudo-religious B-grade horror flicks to know that luxuriant facial hair and a predilection for smocks are definitely a red flag. Some have argued that the religious fervour that fuelled his art was responsible for his unhealthy dynamic with sex. Maybe. Let's just say the Catholic Church knows a lot about this dynamic, and Eric Gill is not the only person associated with that institution who did terrible things in secret while professing a deep faith in public.

A portrait of Eric Gill (hopefully having a good long think about his terrible behaviour) with Alice Mary (née Knewstub), Lady Rothenstein, by her husband William Rothenstein.

Like many other designers, we had heard the basic details about Eric Gill being 'a weirdo' for years, and it sounded bad, but we liked the typeface and we used it anyway. Worse, we glossed over it as 'ancient history that doesn't detract from the work' in our typography classes. It wasn't until a distressed student who had actually read the diary entries called us out that we read them ourselves. Big mistake. Trust us on this, don't look it up. You can't unread it.

We will not dwell on Gill's long-suffering wife, sister and children, or the curious incident of the dog in the night-time, any longer. Let's turn to the broader cultural context in which Gill lived and his typeface was created.

A modern typeface for a turbulent time

History tends to focus so much on the two World Wars of the 20th century that the years in between, the 1920s and 30s, seem like just a breathing space. But in fact this time, when Gill was most prolific, was a period of tremendous political, social and economic upheaval. He was politically active as a pacifist, and would have viewed developments in Italy, Spain and Germany leading up to the war with alarm.

Artistically, Eric Gill's life spans Art Nouveau and Art Deco to modernism. His illustrations for *The Four Gospels* are a good example of how dramatic the aesthetic change was over that time period. The book looks like the love child of traditional medieval manuscripts and the

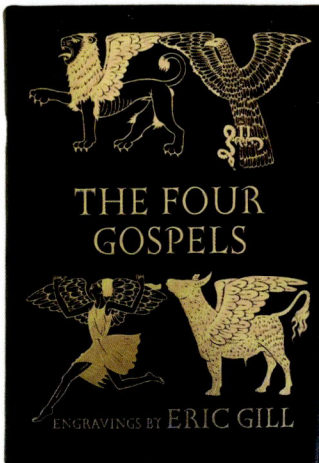

The Four Gospels, opened and ready to sit tastefully on a coffee table in an Art Deco apartment.

1890s illustrations of Aubrey Beardsley (another sexually controversial English artist who converted to Catholicism, just saying). Gothic but streamlined, *The Four Gospels* wouldn't look out of place in the interior of a fancy Art Deco apartment.

Gill Sans was released in 1928 and had been explicitly designed to reflect the new Art Deco styling. Gill was working with the Monotype Corporation, which was ruled over (and we mean *ruled*) by one Stanley 'I have thoughts' Morison.

Morison was looking for a true modern typeface, one that was designed by someone who was still alive. He asked Eric Gill to make a competitor to the newfangled and popular sans serif, geometric-style typefaces like Futura. Morison figured that a typeface similar to the Johnston typeface, made for the London Underground, would be a bestseller. He was right.

People often think Gill Sans *is* the London Underground typeface, but it was actually adopted in 1929 as the corporate typeface for another train service, the London North Eastern Railway (LNER). The easy way to tell Johnston is *not* Gill Sans is that the leg of the 'R' is straight instead of slightly curved, and the tail of the capital 'Q' is shorter.

Stroke modulation

Gill Sans is a sans serif font, categorized as 'Humanist' in the Vox type classification system. This means it uses geometric shapes but is characterized by some stroke modulation (an actual design term, and not what you might be thinking…), making it more organic and less machine-like. This is evident in the lowercase 'a', 'e', 'g' and 'r'.

Another key feature is the vertical stroke ends on letters such as upper- and lowercase 'c' and 's' and the lowercase 'f', which creates the optical illusion of tapering.

(top) The instantly recognizable London Underground logo featuring the Johnston typeface.

(above) Eric Gill in front of the Flying Scotsman, badged by a sign hand-painted by Gill in Gill Sans.

a g e r

stroke modulation

C c S s f

vertical stroke terminals

Gill Sans was designed for both body copy and display text and it includes a quite extensive 36 derivations — a big family of weights and styles, ranging from condensed and thin to heavy.

There's a lot to like about Gill Sans, especially the geometry and the mix of narrow and broad characters. Other sans serif typefaces like Helvetica feature a more uniform width of characters, sure, but that does give a stretched and artificial look to some letters.

We prefer the mix that Gill Sans utilizes, but once you start getting into the bold, extra-bold, ultra-bold and heavy faces, the letterforms look ridiculous. Really, at that point what typeface doesn't? But this one is bad. The letterforms lose all proportions: there's a 'let's see how much air we can pump into these babies before they blow' kind of look. We cannot seriously think of a single instance when we would be tempted to use them. Having said that, you do see Gill Sans Ultra Bold used on comedy film posters. Probably because it does look ridiculous.

The scale between the x-height and the cap height is bothersome. Gill went for a deliberately and comparatively low x-height, and if you look at the letters long enough the uppercase characters tend to teeter over the lowercase ones.

To be really fussy — which we are — some individual letters are also annoying. A successful uppercase 'G' is tough to nail, sure, but in Gill Sans it looks top-heavy, like it's about to topple over. Same with the double-storey (an 'a' with the little curl over the top) lowercase 'a'. Problems that make it hard to set Gill Sans successfully as body copy.

Some designers argue that Gill Sans is not a body copy typeface at all. Having seen one too many student projects trying and failing to use Gill Sans successfully, we are forced to agree. Gill Sans is not great for body copy — or for beginners.

Lorem ipsum
Gill Sans

Lorem ipsum
Helvetica

cap height
x-height

Gill Sans

baseline

Gill Sans

Gill Sans Light

Gill Sans Light Italic

Gill Sans Book

Gill Sans Book Italic

Gill Sans Medium

Gill Sans Medium Italic

Gill Sans Bold

Gill Sans Bold Italic

Gill Sans Heavy

Gill Sans Heavy Italic

Gill Sans Extra Bold

Gill Sans Ultra Bold

Gill Sans Condensed Book

Gill Sans Condensed Book Italic

Gill Sans Condensed Bold

Gill Sans Condensed Ultra Bold

Gill Sans Extra Condensed Bold

Gill Sans Shadow Light

Gill Sans Shadow Medium

GILL SANS SHADOW OUTLINE

Gill Sans

We finally found a professional use for Gill Sans Ultra Bold.

Gill Sans in the wild

Not everyone is hesitant to associate with Gill Sans. The BBC used this typeface in its branding from 1997 to 2017, when it began to be phased out, post-dating the revelations about Eric Gill's personal life. Penguin Books chose Gill Sans for their classic paperback covers in more innocent times, and later stuck by their choice for reissues.

There's a safe and trustworthy feel, a 'keep calm and carry on' vibe about Gill Sans, which in this world is a welcome thing visually. Although it has fallen out of fashion recently, it's still a good choice if you want something conservative but less formal than a geometric serif typeface. Which brings us to the big question in this chapter: given what you now know about its origins, should you change your default typeface to Gill Sans?

Kiss, date, marry or kill?

Knowing the truth about Eric Gill makes some designers uncomfortable about using the Gill Sans typeface. Others can put the associations aside. For us, the magic has gone. The break-up happened slowly but it post-dates reading the diary entries, showing that perhaps you cannot always separate the art from the artist.

Despite any other associations, Gill Sans still has a lot going for it. On a purely aesthetic level it is attractive — elegant, modern and spare — and has a degree of sophistication. Despite how tricky it can be to set well, it's reliable. Most of all, it's very British. Not quirky British, like Benedict Cumberbatch, more of the smooth, good-looking British, like Jude Law. Put it this way, we think you could hold a decent conversation with Gill Sans.

For those of you still dating — or even married to — Gill Sans, we don't judge. It's just that there are other sans serifs in our life now.

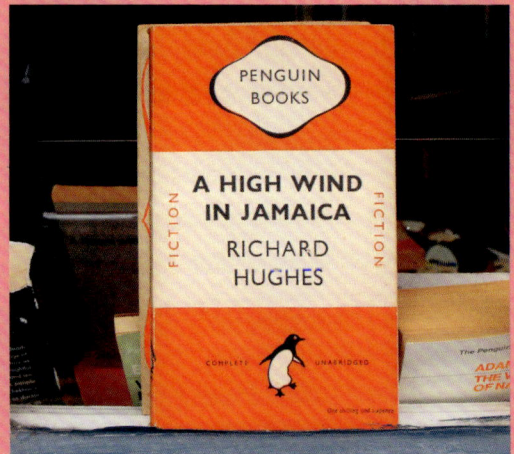

(left) Much of the BBC signage still features Gill Sans but the website doesn't (it started to be replaced by the new Reith typeface across branding in 2017).

(above and opposite) Vintage Penguin cover using Gill Sans, and used more recently on an umbrella.

PELICAN BOOKS
THE WEATHER
GEORGE KIMBLE AND RAYMOND BUSH
PELICAN BOOKS
THE WEATHER
GEORGE KIMBLE AND RAYMOND BUSH

Futura

Designer: Paul Renner
Date: 1927

Portrait of Paul Renner from 1927.

We, like every other graphic designer ever (a bold claim, but we stand by it), went through a Futura phase, a period of intense love where you just want to use Futura for everything and find a way to do it. For some designers this phase is over when they leave design school, for others it's a lifelong battle to put the Futura down.

This devotion is understandable, because why not use Futura for everything? It's clean, it's simple, and most of all it looks like a designer made it. Look, we know that all typefaces are created by designers, but this one looks like it was made by a real designer. One who cared deeply about, and knew how to do, good design. The kind of designer who has a painfully tasteful apartment. With a Barcelona chair.

Futura looks this way because its creator was that kind of designer. More than that, he was a teacher, writer, subversive intellectual and OG Antifa. The story of Futura is the story of modernism and of how typography can be radical. Which means this chapter is about more than the challenges of mathematical proportions in typeface design, although it is about that too.

OG Antifa

Futura was released in 1927 and designed by the German designer Paul Renner. Refreshingly, it was not named after him. Renner was born in Wernigerode, central Germany, in 1878. His father was deeply, evangelically religious, and young Paul was instilled with what's been described as a very German sense of duty.

Renner was a painter, graphic designer and type designer who designed books for a living before becoming a teacher. He was first principal at the Printing Trade School in Munich and then co-founder and director of the Master School for Germany's Printers. His most notable books are *Typographie als Kunst* (*Typography as Art*) and *Die Kunst der Typographie* (*The Art of Typography*), but the publication that got him fired by the Nazis was called *Kulturbolschewismus?* (*Cultural Bolshevism?*), which gives us a clue about his politics.

abcdefghijklm
nopqrstuvwxyz
ABCDEFGHIJKLM
NOPQRSTUVWXYZ
0123456789!?

abcdefghijklm
nopqrstuvwxyz
ABCDEFGHIJKLM
NOPQRSTUVWXYZ
0123456789!?

ß1234567890ABCDEFGHIJKLMNOPQRSTUVXYZAKW

Design drawing of Futura
by Paul Renner.

Futura

You might think that because Futura looks modernist then Paul Renner must have studied or worked at the Bauhaus. Although Futura looks like it was designed at the Bauhaus, Renner wasn't from the Bauhaus, and Futura isn't either. Renner was a friend of, and was influenced by, the Bauhaus, though, and it played a role in his political troubles with the Nazis.

Bauhaus students having a jolly good time and annoying Nazis.

The New Typography – and leather pants

If you've studied design history, you will know that the Bauhaus was an art school that opened in 1919 in Berlin. Its teachers and students were progressives, embracing (and trying to create) the new. The Bauhaus was accused of subversion and 'cultural Bolshevism', and the Nazis shut it down forever in 1933. The 'subversion' was in part because it was the inspiration for a new graphic design style called '*die Neue Typographie*' (the New Typography), and Renner was a major proponent.

Advertisement for Futura in the magazine *Gebrauchsgraphik*, 1929. An example of the New Typography using Futura and an excitingly angled type solution.

DIE
SCHRIFT
UNSERER
ZEIT

FRANKFURT AM MAIN

FUTURA

NIEDERLASSUNGEN IN ALLEN TEILEN DER WELT

Nicht die Anpassung der Letter an die maschinelle Arbeitsweise ist das Entscheidende, sondern daß die Schrift selber den klaren und sauberen Stil der Maschine trägt. - Um das Prinzip allein willen wäre sie höchstens ein interessanter Versuch. Aber in Wahrheit ist sie mehr, nämlich ein sehr geglückter Versuch; sie ist in Wahrheit auch mehr als ein neues und ausdrucksloses Maschinen-produkt, nämlich eine Schrift von bestimmtem Ausdruckswert. Es gibt viele Antiqua-Grotesk-schriften, die an technischer Vereinfachung der Futuraschrift kaum nachstehen, dagegen keine, die ihr an klassischer Reinheit des Satzbildes gleichkommt. - Das Bemerkenswerte an dieser Schrift ist nicht der Versuch der Reduktion der Buchstaben auf abstrakte Formelemente, sondern daß das Schriftbild im Ganzen trotz den abstrakten Formen im Einzelnen einen harmo-nischen und doch nicht langweiligen Charakter trägt. / Hermann Herrigel im »Kunstwart«

mager
halbfett
und fett

BAUERSCHE
GIESSEREI

Blackletter (also known as gothic) type is the very traditional Germanic type found in old bibles, biker gang tattoos and the logo of *The New York Times*.

The Nazis hated the New Typography because it called for using Latin (or roman) sans serifs instead of blackletter letterforms. In their opinion, blackletter type was the only kind that should be used because, well, it always had been. The Nazis literally branded themselves with blackletter, making it a signifier of 'good German culture'. Like everything then (and now), seemingly non-political things could become the subject of political arguments. Renner had strong views, and the arguments got heated; he hit the Nazis where it hurt when he declared blackletter akin to lederhosen, calling it 'a nostalgic leftover, the displaced remains of an earlier age'.

The Nazis really liked wearing lederhosen

Renner lost his job as director of the Master School in 1933 for defending fellow type designer Jan Tschichold, who had been taken into 'protective custody'. The Nazis accused Renner of 'intellectual subversion' and for using Latin typeforms, 'an imbalance that could not be politically justified'. Which just goes to show that fascists can get annoyed about anything, not just who can use what bathroom.

Renner's 1932 booklet *Cultural Bolshevism?* is what really did him in. The design was radical, but the content was the real problem. Renner directly took aim at the Nazis' art and culture policies, writing: 'One day the ever more malicious and violent political idiocy will be able to sweep away the entire Western culture with its dirty sleeve.' In these days of endless culture wars, we totally get what he was on about there.

Renner is described by those who knew him as not having much time for the 'modern culture', abstract art, jazz, cinema, dancing and the like. He admired modernism because it was functional, not because it was radical. In his words, typography should be 'returned to its true function of being read'.

Renner's son-in-law once said about him: 'A day when he did nothing, at least read nothing serious, was for him a day sadly lost', which makes him maybe not that much fun at dinner parties. Getting kicked out of your job for taking a stand on Latin geometric sans serifs makes you a legitimate Antifa though, and we would for sure invite him to our parties.

We imagine him as Captain von Trapp in *The Sound of Music*, a conservative guy, but not an intolerant Nazi conservative guy. Unlike Jan Tschichold (and Captain von Trapp), Renner wasn't forced to flee the Nazis for Switzerland. He lived in internal exile and died in Hödingen in 1956. Renner held strong views about the politics of design for the rest of his life, declaring, for instance, that he didn't like the later German taste for large books because he thought that was the kind of vanity that got the country into trouble to begin with.

Form follows function and so follows Futura

Futura was commissioned in 1924 by the Austrian publisher Jakob Hegner, who wanted a typeface that was 'artistically liberating'. Futura is similar to Renner's earlier typeface, Renner, which uses a dot where the stem of the r should be and has an excitingly zigzaggy lowercase 'g'.

Renner's 1932 pamphlet against the Nazi cultural policy *Kulturbolschewismus?* (Cultural Bolshevism?). The title is set in Futura Display.

ABGRŒars KLMNO
vwxchck!?
XYZÆŒ
ÇØ$ÅÖÜ
aabcdefgghijklmmnno
pqrsſtuvwxyzchckﬀﬁﬂ
ﬃﬄﬆßßæœøçr
1234567890
1234567890
.,-:;!?'«»(*§†
ˊˋˆ¨ ˜˚
Bschckx

Renner worked on Futura between 1924 and 1926, and it was released commercially by the Bauer Type Foundry in 1927. Futura was an instant success, and was consequently widely ripped off, but it wasn't the first geometric-style sans serif typeface released. Edward Johnston's typeface for the London Underground and the typeface Erbar were already out, but Renner claimed that he had the idea for this kind of typeface first. He pointed to a slide show he had taken around, 'telling the whole world what had led me to this new type form', as evidence. Given the kind of straight-up guy he was, we will give him the benefit of the doubt on that one.

It might not have been the first geometric sans serif, but Futura was the first smash hit of its kind. Around the world designers started to use it for all the reasons they still do: it's clear and readable. This is where we get to why the Nazis stopped performatively hating Latin sans serifs.

The Nazis had forced the city of Hanover to redo all its street signage from Futura back to blackletter in 1934, but in 1943 Hanover went back to using a Latin typeface (just not Futura). By then the Nazis had realized that Latin letters made street signs much easier to read, which is handy in a war. Propaganda needs to be easily read and understood too. In 1941 Hitler denounced blackletter as 'a Jewish abomination' — because of course he did — so the Nazis did a 180-degree turn and stopped dissing Futura. In fact, they had been using Futura for a while, notably in 1933, the same year they forced Renner out of his job.

The publication *Mitteilungsblatt der Reichsdeutschen in Rumänien* (*Newsletter of Germans of the Reich in Romania*) – we are betting zero stars on Amazon – two ways: a 1940 edition (top) and a 1944 edition (above) after the Nazis gave up on people outside of Germany being able to easily read blackletter type.

(left) An invitation to a 'book burning event' from 1933, showing the Nazis were using Futura for a long time.

(opposite) Drafts of Futura showing chunky alternative letterforms of the 'a', 'r' and 'g', reminiscent of Paul Renner's previous typeface, Renner.

r m

subtle stroke modulation

Some of the curved strokes taper ever so slightly where they join the vertical strokes.

a b

bowls not perfectly circular

Several of the optically 'perfect' looking circles actually aren't, like the bowls of the 'a' and 'b'.

Mathematical proportions (but not really)

Futura is a 'Lineal Geometric' in the Vox classification system. 'Geometric' means typefaces based on mathematical shapes: full circles and vertical strokes (theoretically) without stroke modulation. The strokes in Futura look like they are the same width all the way around, but there are some weighted strokes and non-perfect circles.

Renner made these choices because designing by maths to make purely geometric forms isn't designing for the human eye. Sometimes in design we are faced with a choice between being *optically* correct — which looks right — and being *mathematically* correct — which looks wrong. With Futura, Renner walks this tightrope with absolute confidence.

The renowned typographer Robert Bringhurst, in *The Elements of Typographic Style*, says that Futura can be set as extended text. Which is pushing it a little bit, in our opinion. Futura doesn't always read very well as small body copy because of the straightness of some of the letters, like the lowercase 'j', and the big differences in the width of the letterforms.

Having said that, the combination of wide and narrow letterforms does reflect our alphabet. Think about when you handwrite: some letters are broad and some are very narrow. The letterform widths in Futura actually reflect the proportions of classical roman capitals, even if they look extreme. Other sans serif typefaces — Helvetica, for example — make much more of an attempt to regulate the width of the letterforms, and look more forced and artificial. Futura more closely follows typographic tradition, which is very on-brand for Paul Renner.

Futura has more horizontal variation in the width between letters than Helvetica, which makes more of an effort to suppress itself. The straight lowercase 'j' and the backwards/upside-down s-shaped question mark are other distinctive features of Futura.

mijo?

Futura

mijo?

Helvetica

Is Futura fun?

Some type websites use 'fun' as a classification to help people find the right typeface. Futura is not fun. Futura is more like Paul Renner at a dinner party, serious. Like modernist architecture, Futura is relentlessly style over comfort. We think of Futura as being like the Barcelona chair: it looks great, but it is uncomfortable, and also — is it for one person or two? (Which is kind of how we feel about Futura's 'o' being so wide and the 'j' being so straight and thin.)

Futura was originally released in six weights. Futura Black was added much later, and it looks different, more stencil-like. Futura Bold is far and away the best font of all the Futuras. Futura Ultra Light is way too weedy and should never be used — it's not good at either large sizes or really small ones. Overall, the proportions and the integrity of each character are consistent through all the different weights, even the condensed faces. Quite an achievement by Renner, as many other typefaces fall flat in this regard.

Type specimen from 1938 showing a range of Futura weights available (but not Futura Ultra Light).

Futura in the wild

Although we quibble with some of the letterforms (we prefer our lowercase 'j' to have a curl in the tail, and the question mark is a bit bonkers), we can't help but admire the simplicity and economy of Futura's forms. Many designers agree. In a world filled with sans serifs, Futura is still widely used.

Stanley Kubrick used sans serifs for just about every film, regardless of what it was about. According to the designer and one-time assistant to Kubrick, Tony Frewin, Kubrick's favourite typeface was Futura Extra Bold. Frewin tried to turn Kubrick away from sans serifs with no luck (sympathies to you Tony, clients can be annoying like that).

Futura was arguably overused in the 1980s. People talk of the 80s as being the era of big hair and big shoulder pads, forgetting that the late 80s were also a time of very generous letterspacing. Futura is a typeface that can handle a lot of letterspacing and remain cohesive enough to be readable. We are still fond of this aspect of Futura, but we do understand why a full-page ad was taken out in 1992 by the 'Art Directors Against Futura Extra Bold Condensed' in *Typography 13: The Annual of the Type Directors Club* calling for a boycott.

Futura still has lots of fans though. When IKEA switched from Futura to Verdana in 2009 for their catalogues and website it ignited something of a type war, and not just among designers, but normal people too. So, if you are still in your Futura phase should you, like IKEA, ditch it as your default typeface?

Kiss, date, marry or kill?

We had our Futura phase in design school but we have used it less and less in our professional lives. These days we can even admit that Verdana is in some ways better than Futura. Certainly, Verdana is a better choice for your default email typeface. Some people think Futura looks juvenile, and we agree it does in that context.

Futura can be hard to work with too, and sometimes we have to stop using it for a while. Then we use it and fall in love all over again. You just can't go past Futura when you need to complement a classic serif font — sort of like the pairing between a crisp wine and a rich cheese.

So maybe we are married. Yes, it is ubiquitous, and probably overused, but whenever we see it we don't think, 'Oh Futura, AGAIN?' (which is usually our response to Helvetica). Maybe we continue to love it because the very first words Paul Renner set in Futura, *'Die schrift unserer zeit'* (the font of our time), are true. For a typeface that is almost a hundred years old, it still looks modern, and maybe it always will.

(above) IKEA: the unwitting instigator of a type war when they changed the text they used for their catalogues. The logo uses a commissioned version of Futura called IKEA Sans.

(left) Food and drink companies like Futura too, including Absolut Vodka and Domino's Pizza.

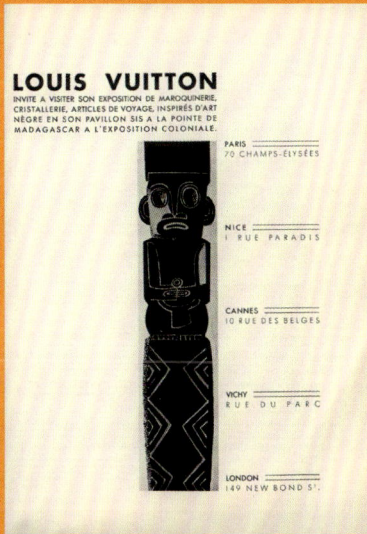

(top) Retail giant Costco uses a custom Futura Italic for its logo.

(above) Louis Vuitton has used Futura for a long time – this ad is from 1931.

(top right) Futura was a good pick for the type for the poster of Kubrick's movie *2001: A Space Odyssey*, because a year later it was chosen to be used in space, literally.

(right) Futura became the first typeface on the moon when it was used for the 'We came in peace for all mankind' lunar plaque in 1969.

Bodoni

Designer: Giovanni Battista Bodoni
Date: 1790

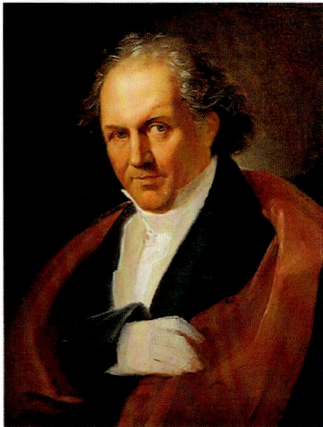

Portrait of Bodoni by Giuseppe Lucatelli, 1805–6, Parma, Museo Glauco Lombardi.

At the age of 28, Giovanni Bodoni scored a Very Important Job working as Director of the Royal Press for the Duke of Parma. At that age, no one was making us director of anything. We were still busy being barked at by various bosses and clients to make the type bigger and bolder and to 'try that bit centred'.

We thought that Bodoni scored this gig because he was nicer to his bosses than we were. He probably never told the duke, 'Don't even ask me to put that type in a starburst' like we did to our boss, Deb (sorry Deb). Turns out that Bodoni was connected and prodigiously talented.

So, grab your sunscreen and a bottle of prosecco, as we are off to the Mediterranean for the story of typography's first rockstar.

Talented (and connected)

Giovanni Battista Bodoni (Giambattista to his friends) was born in 1740 in the Italian town of Saluzzo in what was the Duchy of Parma. He was the son of a printer at a time when you were encouraged to follow in your father's footsteps. In the 1700s you went where the patronage was, so in 1758 young Bodoni upped stakes and moved to Rome. Bodoni had planned to visit his typographic inspiration, John Baskerville, in London but fell ill on the way and had to turn back. So, they never met.

Back in Rome, and feeling better, Bodoni began working for the Sacra Congregatio de Propaganda Fide, the missionary arm of the Vatican, which still exists today. Now known as the Congregation for the Evangelization of Peoples (catchy), it translates Christian texts into many languages to spread the holy word. Here Bodoni worked on Greek, Ethiopian, Illyrian, Bulgarian, Armenian, English, Persian, Arabic, Hebrew, Albanian and Irish texts. His bosses, Cardinal Giuseppe Spinelli and Costantino Ruggieri, noticed that he was easily able to sort all sorts of sorts (the non-Latin ones, anyway) while he was cleaning them. Sensing a talent for languages, they sent him to the prestigious Collegio della Sapienza to study Hebrew and Arabic. When he came back, Bodoni specialized in compositing foreign language books.

Bodoni

abcdefghijklm
nopqrstuvwxyz
ABCDEFGHIJKLM
NOPQRSTUVWXYZ
0123456789!?

abcdefghijklm
nopqrstuvwxyz
ABCDEFGHIJKLM
NOPQRSTUVWXYZ
0123456789!?

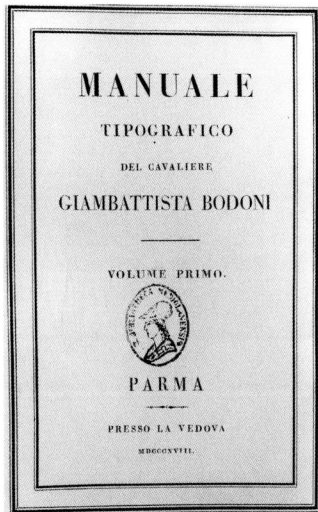

MANUALE

TIPOGRAFICO

DEL CAVALIERE

GIAMBATTISTA BODONI

VOLUME PRIMO.

PARMA

PRESSO LA VEDOVA

MDCCXVIII.

The *Manuale Tipografico*; the modern-day reprints are a great addition to any designer's library.

Then (and some would argue now) the Catholic Church operated as much like a multinational corporation as a religious institution. Bodoni's bosses in Rome helped him land his next gig in 1768, when he was appointed director of the Stamperia Reale (the Royal Press). This was a prestigious start-up run by Ferdinand I, the Duke of Parma, and his minister Guillaume du Tillot. When Bodoni was appointed, the Royal Press was just an idea, and he had to construct the press, order type from Pierre-Simon Fournier in France, make the tools and get all the ink and paper in time for the official launch; it sounds a bit stressful.

You're probably thinking, Parma, wasn't that the town where they spent their time perfecting delicious, crumbed chicken dishes? (Look it up, the Chicken Parma is a celebrated Australian pub staple, and the rest of the world should not miss out.) Well, yes, but both Ferdinand and Guillaume wanted to liberalize and improve the Duchy, because they were minor exponents of the Enlightenment. Guillaume was the brains of the operation and famous for promoting French musical theatre and the cultivation of the potato — both with the aim of bettering society.

The press was Tillot's idea for fostering education and culture, and it worked. Bodoni's talent and skill is credited with making Palma into the world centre of printing, and he became a celebrity and tourist attraction. Visitors used to hang around at his print shop hoping to see him at work. Fellow printer (with a side hustle as Founding Father of the US) Benjamin Franklin once wrote him a fan letter. When Napoleon took over Parma and the duke (mysteriously, but perhaps not surprisingly) suddenly died, things still worked out fine, as Napoleon was a fan of Bodoni. Napoleon and Josephine made the effort to come to Bodoni's workshop one day, but he was sick with gout so they visited him at home instead. This was a sign of great respect: Napoleon didn't make many house calls.

Bodoni had rockstar fame and all the medals and awards, and he made rockstar money too. In 1782 he became Royal Typographer for Charles III of Spain, which came with a life pension, and in 1807 he was exempted from paying taxes for being a 'supreme artist'. He received a second life pension in 1808 from another client, Napoleon's brother-in-law Joachim Murat, and then *another* from Napoleon in 1810 for 'making good progress in the art of typography'.

Bodoni was headhunted so often by other patrons that the duke gave him a private press to keep him at the Royal Press in Parma. He stayed, building up his fan base and presumably turning away other hopeful patrons, until he died in Parma in 1813. Bodoni's death was announced by the ringing of Parma cathedral's largest bell (which was kind of a big deal), and everyone who was anyone attended his funeral.

Bodoni was survived by his much younger widow Margherita (they married when he was 51 and she was 18). Margherita carried on the press and in 1818 she posthumously completed and published Bodoni's catalogue and masterpiece *Manuale Tipografico*. This book took 40 years to create and includes 125 capital letters, 181 Greek and 'oriental' types, 1,036 flourishes, 31 contours and 20 pages of characters and musical symbols. The *Manuale Tipografico* has been called the ultimate designer's specimen book, and you can still buy reprints online.

Bodoni continues to be a tourist attraction, as in 1963 the city of Parma opened a museum in his honour.

A modern typeface

Bodoni the typeface first appeared around 1790. Bodoni was influenced by type designers François-Ambroise, Firmin Didot and Pierre-Simon Fournier, who was in turn influenced by John Baskerville. At the time this style of typography was called 'classical' but looks decidedly modern and is now officially called 'Modern'.

Bodoni required a high degree of precision to print because of the extreme contrast between thick and thin line weights. Metal type was still cast by hand, and technically it was not easy to make those hairline widths. Contemporary accounts reflect how impressive everyone thought Bodoni's achievement was at the time.

Arguably, the typeface Bodoni wouldn't have existed without the improvements in paper manufacturing that were happening in Parma at the time. Rough surfaces are not kind to fine lines. With smoother paper Bodoni could develop a sparser, cleaner page layout. Less overt decoration and more white space brought the typography into sharp focus. Bodoni is a typeface from the Age of Reason and is both recognizably

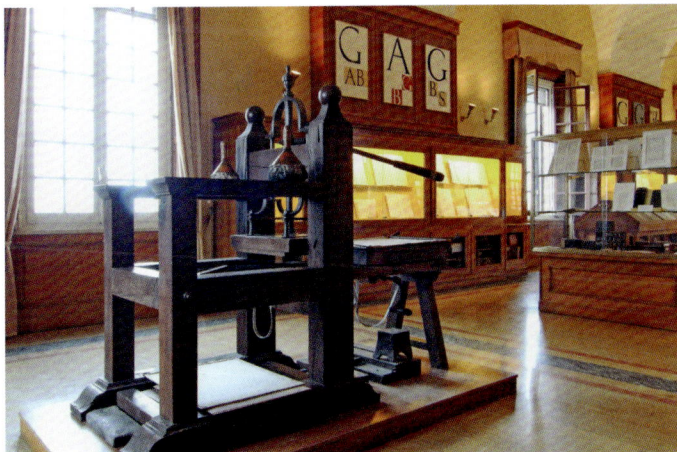

A printing press by Giambattista Bodoni in the Bodoni Museum in Parma.

modern and a reflection of its time. The Enlightenment was a broad philosophical movement of progressive and rational ideas. Its thinkers emphasized scientific methods and questioned religious orthodoxy, and very much wanted to distinguish themselves from everything that had gone on before.

Your average person did not move in the elevated circles Bodoni frequented, nor did they read the congratulatory, 'I say, well spotted, sir!' kind of correspondence that was criss-crossing Europe and America at the time. Nevertheless, ideas spread through salons and the new coffee houses, often via the printed word in the form of pamphlets and journals.

Dazzling Bodoni

Bodoni is classified as 'Didone' under the Vox classification system and is a serif typeface with narrow serifs that are a nearly constant width when horizontal. Some strokes end in a ball terminal instead of the wedge used by many serif typefaces. You see this on the lowercase 'f' and 'j'.

The most distinctive feature — you could call it the 'signature look' — of the Bodoni typeface is the strong contrast between the weight of the thick, predominantly vertical strokes and the very fine, mainly horizontal strokes.

f f
Bodoni   *Times New Roman*

Bodoni ball terminals

j j
Bodoni   *Times New Roman*

Lorem ipsum
Bodoni

Lorem ipsum
Times New Roman

Fashion-favourite Didot, close relation to Bodoni in the Didone family, used in the masthead of *Vogue* magazine

If you've ever flicked through magazines like *Elle* or *Vogue*, you'll recognize that Bodoni belongs to a group of typefaces synonymous with the world of fashion. Although *Elle* and *Vogue* use Didot rather than Bodoni for their mastheads, the family relationship is obvious.

Bodoni set as body copy can be off-putting, but it is more readable than it appears at first glance. Although we are half convinced that fashion magazines and websites that use Bodoni and other Didone typefaces don't expect anyone to actually read their articles (except for *Teen Vogue*, which has great articles).

In the 1940s Bodoni was one of the few typefaces that passed the most popular research method of legibility: the 'blink test'. The blink test was exactly what it sounds like, the number of extra times you blink when reading a passage of text — a somewhat reductive way to think about legibility. In the 1970s the Royal College of Art's Readability of Print Research Unit did some more sophisticated tests and found that type with strong distinctive strokes and a greater difference between letters allowed people to digest information more quickly. Which would explain Bodoni's better-than-expected readability.

Bodoni (and all the Didones really) are best on a white page, or on a field of colour rather than over an image. On a high-contrast background the thin strokes can drop out, leaving sort of half-letters that are still legible from a distance but are a bit odd-looking. The technical term for the effect of dominant thick strokes and receding thin strokes in body copy is 'dazzling'. Which sounds like the most flattering form of criticism.

Bodoni in the wild

Bodoni instantly conveys 'high-class' and 'fashion' and this means it has a very strong 'flavour'. Consequently, Bodoni has a highly strung look to it, and we feel obliged to suck in our stomach whenever we see it. Typefaces from the century after were thicker and bolder, as if designers wanted to throw out all the delicate and refined typefaces of the past. But maybe everyone just got sick of typefaces that looked like they were on a diet all the time?

Bodoni is used by fashion and beauty brands including Elizabeth Arden, Giorgio Armani and the unmistakable lowercase 'c', uppercase 'K' combo of the monogram for Calvin Klein. Because of its fashion associations, Bodoni does often represent the pretentious and the frivolous: we're looking at you, *The Hollywood Reporter*. Because Bodoni is often used to convey elegance and sophistication, another way to work with it is with the deepest sense of irony. This is probably the reason grunge rock icons Nirvana adopted it for their band logo.

Kiss, date, marry or kill?

We think of Bodoni as the Audrey Hepburn of typefaces. Stylish, thin, can be a total nightmare to work with, but you can still take Bodoni anywhere and it will comport itself well. Bodoni never gets sloppy drunk in a couture dress and falls over a trash can showing everyone its underwear. Well, if it does, it looks good while doing it.

The italic is lovely, and we are very partial to the medium italic. For many designers, Bodoni is not a typeface we can use much unless we do the kind of work that really calls for it. This means we would date Bodoni, while knowing all the time that it is out of our league.

Really, Bodoni is a bit like one of those celebrity crushes. You might fantasize about it, but realistically, how often are you going to get the chance to act on those feelings?

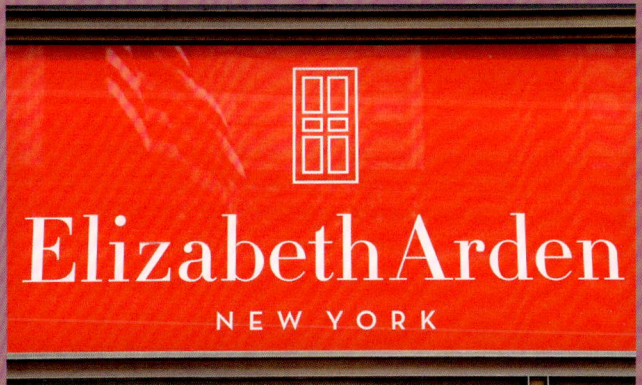

Bodoni is used for the Nirvana logo, *The Hollywood Reporter* masthead, beauty brand Elizabeth Arden, fashion brand Calvin Klein, and the couture house Giorgio Armani.

Goudy

Designer: Frederic W. Goudy
Date: 1915

Portrait of Frederic W. Goudy, 1924.

Designers have the equivalent of an arranged marriage with their employers' corporate typefaces. We are forced to use the same typeface — which we may not like to begin with — over and over again until there's a quickie divorce when we resign.

Goudy Oldstyle was the corporate typeface for Oxford University Press, where we both once worked, and we hated this typeface. When we see it, the loathing we feel rivals that we experience when we see pictures of our ex-boyfriends.

We like Frederic W. Goudy, the designer of Goudy Oldstyle, though. After learning more about him we feel we can let some of the feelings go. We still kind of hate Goudy Oldstyle, but it can get on with its life and we can too. In this spirit, we dedicate this chapter to all survivors of corporate typefaces; we hope you all find the same peace.

Frederic without a 'k'

Frederic W. Goudy was a self-taught printer, typographer and type designer, former bookkeeper and son of a real estate business owner. There's no 'k' in Frederic, by the way. Fred once said, 'Someday I'll design a typeface without a 'k' in it, and then let's see the bastards misspell my name.'

Frederic-with-no-k was born in Bloomington, Illinois, in 1865 — right at the end of the American Civil War. As a kid he pored over *Harper's Weekly* magazine in the library and learned how to accurately trace in pencil and use a pantograph to enlarge and replicate illustrations. Goudy claimed his typeface designs were drawn freehand, without the use of a straight edge, a pair of compasses, or even a French curve. Amazing, if true; and it probably is true — he had lots of practice.

At the age of 28 Fred left his job as a bookkeeper with his dad's business and moved to Chicago. Here he became a copywriter and art director, creating advertisements for local printers. In his 30s, Goudy reinvented himself as a fine printer. Working in advertising can do that to a designer — make you want to create things that people actually

abcdefghijklm
nopqrstuvwxyz
ABCDEFGHIJKLM
NOPQRSTUVWXYZ
0123456789!?

abcdefghijklm
nopqrstuvwxyz
ABCDEFGHIJKLM
NOPQRSTUVWXYZ
0123456789!?

ABCDEFGHIJKLMN
OPQRSTUVWXYZ&

ABCDEFGHIJKLMNOPQRS
TUVWXYZ&fifffiflffl.,';:!?-
abcdefghijklmnopqrst
uvwxyz$1234567890

(above) An original printed sample of Goudy Oldstyle.

(right) Frederic Goudy's wife and fellow printer Bertha Sprinks Goudy.

love and want to keep. Goudy fell in love with the art of printing too, saying that after he became 'inoculated' with printers' ink he was never the same again. He worked with type for years, but only started designing typefaces at the age of 46.

Inspired by the Kelmscott Press, which was founded by William Morris in the late 19th century and kickstarted the fine press movement, Goudy co-founded The Village Press in 1903 with his wife Bertha Sprinks Goudy, and fellow bookkeeper Will Ransom (who would go on to be a designer and creator of the Parsons series of typefaces — but not Ransom, as you'd be forgiven for thinking). Their first book from The Village Press was *Printing*, an essay by the Arts & Crafts heroes William Morris and Emery Walker. Will left the business after an unprofitable first year, and the Goudys moved The Village Press first to Massachusetts then to New York City. In 1908 the press sadly burned to the ground and the Goudys started over again, moving the press several more times.

In 1924 they finally settled what was now The Village Press and Foundry into a converted water mill next to their house in Marlboro, New York. Sadly, yet another equally devastating fire in 1939 burned the workshop down and much of their personal collection was lost.

In the grand tradition of type history, you've probably never heard of Goudy's wife, Bertha. She was the principal typesetter and ran the business of The Village Press for 32 years. In 1933 *Time* magazine called her 'the world's ablest woman printer' (they could have just called her a 'printer', there are no 'man printers'). We think her contribution, especially in keeping everything running, somewhat explains Goudy's prodigious output of 123 typefaces and 59 publications. Goudy himself, who rarely turned down a speaking engagement, was famously good at self-promotion.

Goudy's other typefaces include Copperplate Gothic, Italian Old Style, Berkeley Old Style and Kennerley. He took his time to name a typeface after Bertha — he named Deepdene after their house first. He finally called his 100th design Bertham — which is… not the *loveliest* typeface name.

Goudy was commissioned by the American Type Founders Company (ATF) to design Goudy Oldstyle in 1915, and it was intended to be a good all-round typeface. Several variations followed, some created by other designers. Although the typeface was quite lucrative for ATF, Goudy received no royalties — he had sold his original design for US$1500 — and his relationship with ATF soured as a result. After that, Goudy often, unsuccessfully and at great personal cost, sued to protect the licensing of his typefaces.

The logo for *The Village Press* shows the Arts & Crafts influence and medieval vibe.

Goudy was appointed art director to Lanston Monotype in 1920. In 1927 he became vice president of the Continental Type Founders Association, which distributed most of his typefaces. Goudy taught design from 1916 to 1929, and he seems to have been a good teacher: accounts of his classes make us wish he had taught us.

Fred had a reputation for fast cars and girls. We couldn't verify this, but everyone seems to agree that the short, plump exterior of the man didn't match the person within. We think he was one of the fun designers. He certainly had some of the best one-liners: our favourite is, 'All the old fellows stole our best ideas' (because it's true). Another is his aphorism for a type crime: 'A man that would letterspace lowercase would steal sheep' ('steal' is the family-friendly version).

Fred wasn't universally liked, perhaps from professional jealousy of his commercial success and definitely for his design sensibility. Printer Daniel Berkeley Updike once snidely wrote that Goudy never got over wanting to make medieval books. Not wrong: it doesn't get more 'olde worlde' than using the word 'village' for your business and naming your first typeface Camelot. Designer W.A. Dwiggins (who coined the term 'graphic design') was a student and friend, but admitted that Goudy's work lacked 'snap' and 'acidity'. Stanley Morison once wrote to a friend that he was glad Times New Roman didn't look like Fred Goudy had designed it. Ouch.

Goudy complained late in his life that he was left behind at the end of his career. But he was always Arts & Crafts in a century of sans serifs, and not all of his typefaces aged well. Goudy Oldstyle certainly didn't. He died in 1947 at the age of 82.

An unwanted restlessness

As the name suggests, Goudy Oldstyle is classified as 'Old Style' within the Vox classification system. It belongs to the Garalde subcategory, which features lowercase 'e's with a horizontal crossbar. Garaldes have slightly more contrast between the thick and thin strokes than their humanist cousins, which tend to have an angled crossbar on the 'e'.

Goudy Oldstyle has a hand-drawn feel; the thick and thin strokes in the capitals vary in weight between letters. In what we think is the worst feature, some of the serifs have the appearance of a slight curve or dip in the middle.

Type designer Walter Tracy described Goudy as being too fond of an 'e' with an angled crossbar, or a 'tilted centre', because it was common in 15th-century printing. Tracy felt the crossbar added an 'unwanted restlessness' to many of Goudy's type designs. It doesn't have a tilted crossbar, but we think the slight curves make Goudy Oldstyle almost bouncy, and there is indeed an unwanted restlessness about it.

Goudy Oldstyle   Centaur

horizontal crossbar on Goudy 'e'

curve on serifs

A close examination leads us to believe Fred Goudy's claim that he drew typefaces by hand. But overall, and we hate to say it, Goudy Oldstyle is objectively quite a good-looking typeface (if you like that kind of thing, of course).

Most characters in Goudy Oldstyle are quite broad, but the stroke weights in the roman face are relatively fine. Which makes it a good choice if you need to save space with a slab of text, as it won't look too dense on the page. We found this out against our will at Oxford University Press.

Goudy Oldstyle has a true italic face, not just roman letters forced on a slant (called 'obliques'). Goudy said he modelled the italic on the great italics of the 16th century, which had little or no inclination but still retained that character. A sense of calligraphy is evoked by the tail of the capital 'Q' and the diamond-shaped dots on the lowercase 'i' and 'j'. Fun type-nerd fact: these dots are called 'tittles'.

We must give a shout-out to the Goudy Oldstyle italic ampersand, which is one of the most riotous examples you are ever likely to see. Despite our Goudy-induced trauma, we are here for it.

One notable aspect of Goudy Oldstyle is the comparatively short descenders, which give the typeface a bit of a stumpy look. This was an alteration made by ATF to allow for a tighter line setting. Goudy hated it, and that was another reason they parted ways. Who among us has not left a relationship because it was stunting us?

i j

diamond-shaped tittles

Q

calligraphic flourish

  &   &

Oldstyle roman   *Oldstyle italic*

Lorem ipsum

Oldstyle roman

Lorem ipsum

Oldstyle italic

cap height

x-height

baseline

Goudy

Goudy in the wild

Educational institutions love Goudy Oldstyle, and many have made it their corporate typeface. Oxford University Press dates back to 1586, and Goudy Oldstyle does look like it could have been designed then so the choice to make Goudy their corporate typeface makes perfect sense.

The American apparel company J. Crew has previously used Goudy Oldstyle for their company logo. The typeface has even had its Hollywood moments: Ridley Scott alternated the decidedly un-futuristic Goudy Oldstyle with Impact and Helvetica in the opening credits of his sci-fi noir classic *Blade Runner*.

Australian readers will be pleased to learn that Goudy Sans Bold Italic is used in the branding of the famous Australian ice cream treat, the caramelly delicious and yes-they-really-did-name-it-that Golden Gaytime.

Kiss, date, marry or kill?

Many serif typefaces are timeless, but Goudy Oldstyle isn't, and that's the problem. It feels like it belongs to an old-fashioned world that never existed. Like Heath Ledger in the movie *A Knight's Tale*, Goudy Oldstyle might be good-looking and dressed up to look medieval, but it is totally not. There is an 'unwanted restlessness' about it — just like there is in jousting scenes set to Queen's 'We Will Rock You'.

We can both safely say that as designers we haven't looked back since the divorce. We won't ever use Goudy Oldstyle (even if we can objectively see that, like our ex-boyfriends, it is still quite good-looking). Stop being good-looking, Goudy Oldstyle! Because we are never, ever getting back together!

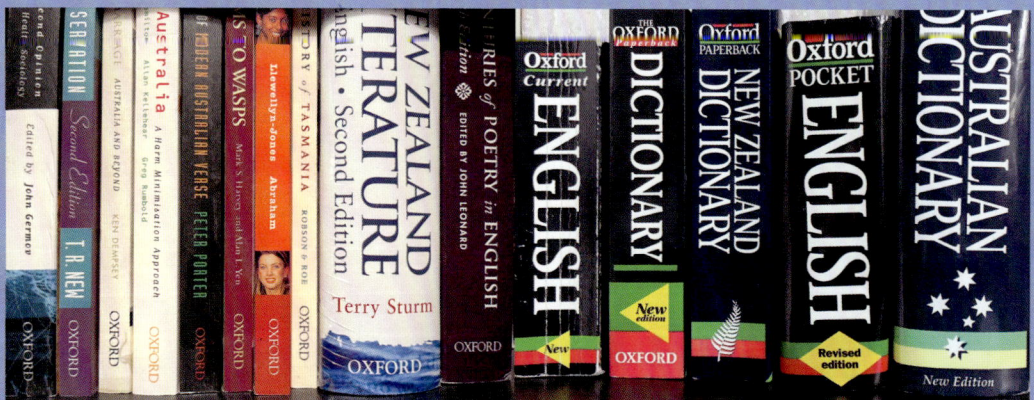

Early in the 21st Century, THE TYRELL CORPORATION advanced Robot evolution into the NEXUS phase — a being virtually identical to a human — known as a *Replicant.*

The NEXUS 6 *Replicants* were superior in strength and agility, and at least equal in intelligence, to the genetic engineers

(above) One of the many educational institutions that use Goudy. The neighbouring Rochester Institute of Technology has an annual speech and award named for Frederic Goudy, but sadly it does not use a Goudy-designed typeface for its branding.

(far left) Goudy trying to be ominous in the opening credits for *Blade Runner.*

(above left) Goudy promising a delicious snack on the Golden Gaytime packaging.

(left) J.Crew store signage.

(opposite) Some of the many book spines upon which we relentlessly had to set the word 'Oxford' in Goudy while working at Oxford University Press.

Baskerville

Designer: John Baskerville
Date: 1750s

Portrait of John Baskerville from the 1914 biography by Josiah H. Benton, who claimed that Baskerville liked colourful clothes and gold lace.

First-year design students are not to be trusted, for they often do bad things with type. This is why we were only allowed to use six typefaces for our first-year assignments at design school. One of the few permitted typefaces was Baskerville.

Ah Baskerville, how we love/hate you. Like an old flatmate, we might have liked you if we hadn't been made to live with you. We don't know if Baskerville is still forced on design students, but in our opinion it should be — if we had to suffer, why shouldn't the young people?

Our teachers made us use Baskerville because it's a classic: clean, simple, accessible and legible, all the things its creator intended it to be. However, the passage of centuries has worn away the other associations attached to Baskerville: atheism, adultery and too much gold lace-wearing.

Yes, there was a Baskerville who made the typeface Baskerville

John Baskerville was born in 1705 in Wolverley, Worcestershire, in the UK. In 1726 he moved to Birmingham to become a writing master (calligraphy teacher), but by then he was already a skilled engraver and stone-cutter known for his highly crafted tombstones. The one surviving engraving is very beautiful (see over the page), demonstrating an impressive skill set for a 17-year-old.

While working in Birmingham, Baskerville started a side hustle making 'japanned' (meaning lacquered, or enamelled) goods, which were very fashionable at the time. Nowadays this sort of cultural appropriation is frowned upon, but this was during the 214 years when Japan heavily restricted trade with the West. Real Japanese goods were very expensive, so there was a market for designer knock-offs, just like there is today.

abcdefghijklm
nopqrstuvwxyz
ABCDEFGHIJKLM
NOPQRSTUVWXYZ
0123456789!?

abcdefghijklmnopqrstuvwxyz
ABCDEFGHIJKLM
NOPQRSTUVWXYZ
0123456789!?

A
SPECIMEN

By *JOHN BASKERVILLE* of *Birmingham*.

I Am indebted to you for two Letters dated from Corcyra. You congratulate me in one of them on the Account you have Received, that I still preserve my former Authority in the Commonwealth: and wish me Joy in the other of my late Marriage. With respect to the First, *if to mean well to the Interest of my Country and to approve that meaning to every Friend of its Liberties, may be consider'd as maintaining my Authority; the Account you have heard is certainly true. But if it consists in rendering those Sentiments effectual to the Public Welfare or at least in daring freely to Support and inforce them;*

I Am indebted to you for two Letters dated from Corcyra. You congratulate me in one of them on the Account you have Received, that I still preserve my former Authority in the Commonwealth: and wish me Joy in the other of my late Marriage. With respect to the first, if to mean well to the Interest of my Country and to approve that meaning to every Friend of its Liberties, may be consider'd as maintaining my Authority; the Account you have heard is certainly true. But if it consists in rendering those Sentiments effectual to the Public Welfare or at least in daring freely to Support and inforce them; alas! my Friend I have not the least sha-

I Am indebted to you for two Letters dated from Corcyra. You congratulate me in one of them on the Account you have received, that I still preserve my former Authority in the Commonwealth: and wish me joy in the other of my late Marriage. With respect to the First, if to mean well to the Interest of my Country and to approve that meaning to every Friend of its Liberties, may be consider'd as maintaining *my Authority; the Account you have heard is certainly true. But if it consists in rendering those Sentiments effectual to the Public Welfare or at least in daring freely to Support and inforce them; alas! my Friend I have not the least shadow of Authority remaining. The Truth of it is, it will be sufficient Honor if I can have so much Authority over myself as to bear with patience our present and impending Calamities: a frame of Mind not to be acquired without difficulty,*

Q. HORATII FLACCI

Hac ego si compellar imagine, cuncta resigno.
Nec somnum plebis laudo satur altilium; nec
Otia divitiis Arabum liberrima muto.
Sæpe verecundum laudasti: rexque, paterque
Audisti coram, nec verbo parcius absens.
Inspice si possum donata reponere lætus.
Haud male Telemachus proles patientis Ulyssei;
Non est aptus equis Ithacæ locus, ut neque planis
Porrectus spatiis, neque multæ prodigus herbæ:
Atride, magis apta tibi tua dona relinquam.
Parvum parva decent. mihi jam non regia Roma,
Sed vacuum Tibur placet, aut imbelle Tarentum.
Strenuus et fortis, causisque Philippus agendis

EPISTOLARUM LIBER I.

Clarus, ab officiis octavam circiter horam
Dum redit, atque foro nimium distare Carinas
Jam grandis natu queritur; conspexit, ut aiunt,
Adrasum quendam vacua tonsoris in umbra
Cultello proprios purgantem leniter ungues.
Demetri, (puer hic non læve jussa Philippi (quis,
Accipiebat) abi, quære, et refer; unde domo,
Cujus fortunæ, quo sit patre, quove patrono.
It, redit, et narrat, Vulteium nomine Menam
Præconem, tenui censu sine crimine notum,
Et properare loco, et cessare, et quærere, et uti
Gaudentem parvisque sodalibus, et lare certo,
Et ludis, et post decisa negotia, Campo.

Baskerville was good at making knick-knacks, or clever in business — or both. Within 10 years he'd made a huge fortune and was able to quit his day job, lease a bunch of land outside the city and build himself a McMansion surrounded by a lovely garden. The delightfully named Easy Hill was a work-from-home situation. Now in his late 40s and pretty wealthy, Baskerville decided to start his own press. Not only did he want to craft the very finest books, but his ambition was also to create the 'best typeface ever'.

One of his best-known printed works was a version of the King James Bible, produced in 1763 after he was appointed printer to Cambridge University. This work set a new standard in quality printing. Your average Gideon Bible gathering dust in a cheap motel drawer diminishes that achievement in modern eyes, but in those days Bible printing was protected by royal privilege. Which makes sense, as you don't want people introducing errors or unauthorized additions to one of the world's important religious texts.

What makes this achievement particularly interesting is that Baskerville is rather famous for being an outspoken atheist (although some argue he was a deist, with a more rationalist belief in a non-interventionist God) who did not like organized religion. To give you an idea of his commitment, he left orders to be buried in unconsecrated land because, as he wrote in his will, 'I have a Hearty Contempt for all Superstition'.

(above left) The surviving example of Baskerville's engraving work.

(above) Baskerville's printing of the King James Bible, showing why you really needed to know your stuff to print a Bible back then.

(opposite) An original specimen of the Baskerville typeface.

AN

INTRODUCTION

TO THE

KNOWLEDGE

OF

MEDALS.

By the late Rev. *DAVID JENNINGS*, D.D.

THE SECOND EDITION.

BIRMINGHAM:
Printed by *SARAH BASKERVILLE;*
And Sold
By JOSEPH JOHNSON, No. 72.
St. Paul's Church Yard.
M DCC LXXV.

QUINTUS

HORATIUS

FLACCUS.

BIRMINGHAMIAE;
Typis S. BASKERVILLE.
MDCCLXXVII.

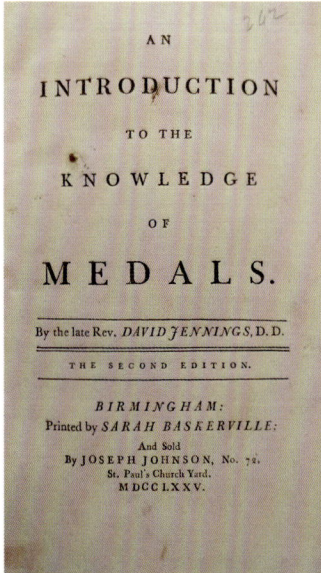

Quintus Horatius Flaccus, and *An Introduction to the Knowledge of Medals*, the two books whose printing is attributed to Sarah Baskerville, formerly Eaves, printed after John Baskerville's death.

Baskerville's epitaph, also specified in his will, reads:

Stranger – Beneath this Cone in Unconsecrated Ground
A Friend to the Liberties of mankind Directed his Body to be Inhum'd
May the Example Contribute to Emancipate thy mind
From the Idle Fears of Superstition
And the wicked arts of priesthood

Atheism, contempt for the church, and conspicuous consumption have lost their shock value today, but it's possible Baskerville's lifestyle might have affected the way his typeface was viewed. The Victorians were scandalized by his apparent atheism. Victorian author Sir Arthur Conan Doyle also lived in Birmingham, and the character of Hugo Baskerville in *The Hound of the Baskervilles* bears a striking resemblance to descriptions of John Baskerville: a show-off, living in defiance of the church teachings, riding around in a tricked-out carriage and wearing too much gold lace.

We are not the only ones who think that Victorian criticisms of the Baskerville typeface as being 'narrow' and 'hurtful to the eyes' may have been influenced by Baskerville's personal life. John Baskerville was a bit of a sly dog in the relationship stakes too, and the Victorians didn't like that either.

Scandal

Around the time he built Easy Hill, Baskerville started a relationship with Sarah Eaves, a married woman with children, whose husband had run off. She was officially his housekeeper but, while accounts vary, either he took Sarah in because she needed a job and their relationship status changed, or she was already his mistress and he moved her in. No one really knows, but they obviously loved each other. Baskerville lived with Sarah openly and scandalously for 10 years until they married, just weeks after her husband finally died.

Sarah Eaves is often described as 'helping to run the print shop'. Back then this was no small undertaking. If the contracts signed by 'printer's devils' (apprentices) are to be believed, HR must have been a nightmare because they are basically all about apprentices promising not to drink excessively.

We choose to believe that Sarah was an equal partner in the business and knew her way around a compositing stick, because she carried on the business for 10 years after Baskerville died. Only two books are directly attributed to her though. As is depressingly usual for this time (and even in our own time), the full extent of this woman's contributions to type history was not recorded.

With Sarah running the workshop, Baskerville was able to concentrate on making 'the best typeface ever', by which he meant a better version of the typeface Caslon. This seems to have been a bit personal.

My typeface is better than your typeface

Caslon is regarded as the first quality typeface to come out of England. Its designer, William Caslon, was the first English printer to successfully 'punch-cut' (carve by hand) letters out of metal. After this, English printers were no longer dependent on European printers to supply them with typefaces, leading one slightly over-enthusiastic biographer to proclaim that William Caslon set England free from what would probably now be called 'European type tyranny'.

Caslon had been around and famous for over 30 years, but if you're going to take someone down, best go for the big guy, right? Baskerville calls Caslon 'an artist' in his preface to his edition of *Paradise Lost* in 1758, where he goes on to give his only public explanation for starting the press, basically saying he can do better than Caslon:

> *Having been an early admirer of the beauty of Letters, I became insensibly desirous of contributing to the perfection of them. I formed to my self Ideas of greater accuracy than had yet appeared, and have endeavoured to produce a Sett of Types according to what I conceived to be their true proportion.*

We admire the flex. These days there might have been threats of cage fights thrown over social media.

Caslon the typeface is more conservative than Baskerville, more modelled after human handwriting. Baskerville is sharper, crisper, more precise and modern. But to be honest, the untrained eye probably finds it hard to distinguish between the two.

Lorem ipsum

Caslon

Lorem ipsum

Baskerville

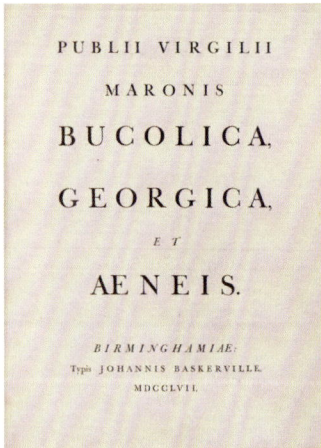

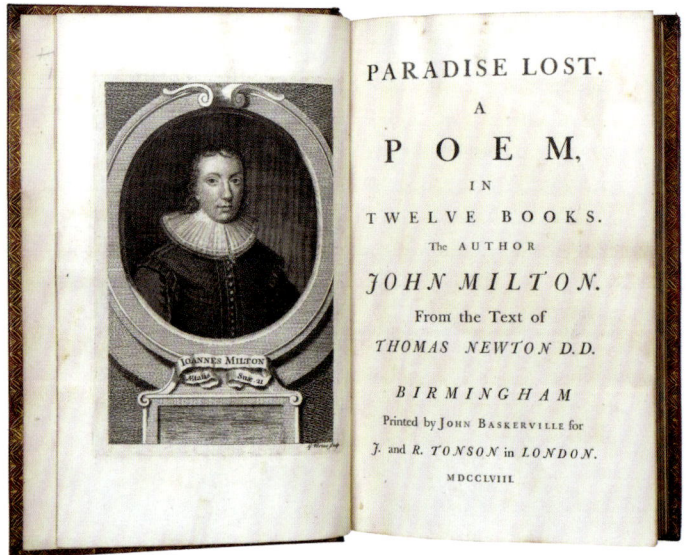

Title pages of *Publii Virgilii Maronis Bucolica, Georgica, et Aeneis* and *Paradise Lost.*

Big in Europe

It took John Baskerville four years to produce Baskerville, and through it all he was always striving for clarity and simplicity. As a result his typographic layouts using Baskerville are more spare, and less decorative, than those that had come before.

Baskerville's career was a classic 'big in Japan' scenario. Baskerville's editions of Lucretius's *De Rerum Natura* and a four-volume set of Ariosto's *Orlando Furioso* were snapped up by Europeans but didn't sell well in England. Baskerville's influence can be seen in the equally famous typeface Bodoni, designed by Italian Giovanni Bodoni. French designer Pierre-Simon Fournier sang his praises in *Manuel typographique* (Manual of Typography) in 1766. The Americans were fans, and fellow printer Benjamin Franklin was a friend.

Baskerville was a perfectionist. He made high-quality books, but they were expensive and the press never made money. Sarah seemed to have a much more pragmatic approach. While she kept the press going after he died, eventually she had to stop and sell all the gear. Not to an English printer though, but to the French dramatist Pierre Beaumarchais, who used it to print an edition of Voltaire. Take that, English-typography-establishment haters!

A night at the mausoleum

Before we look at the anatomy of Baskerville the typeface, it's worth talking about what happened to John Baskerville's own body, because it's pretty wild.

Baskerville died at his beloved Easy Hill in 1775 and was buried in a lead-lined coffin under a mausoleum he built in his backyard. Sarah died in 1788, and their daughter sold the house. Some years later the house was ransacked and burned by rioters (some of whom burned along with it) in the Priestley Riots of 1971. The rioters were fanatics targeting religious dissenters who had supported the French Revolution. Baskerville was long dead by then, but who knows, perhaps memory of his atheism and ties to the French lingered.

A developer bought the estate, pulled down the remains of the house and started cutting a canal through the land. This is how, 46 years later in 1821, workmen found Baskerville's coffin. They opened it up (as you do) and reported that his body was dry, firm and well-preserved, still wrapped in a linen shroud with a branch of laurel. Apparently it was a bit whiffy though, so they closed the coffin up quickly.

Baskerville wouldn't have wanted to be re-buried in consecrated land, but the church refused anyway. Then, as now, you can't just bury a body anywhere, so the coffin sat in a warehouse for eight years and it was reported that the owner would display the body for money. It was opened at least once, because the printer Thomas Underwood made a rather morbid sketch of Baskerville's remains in 1829.

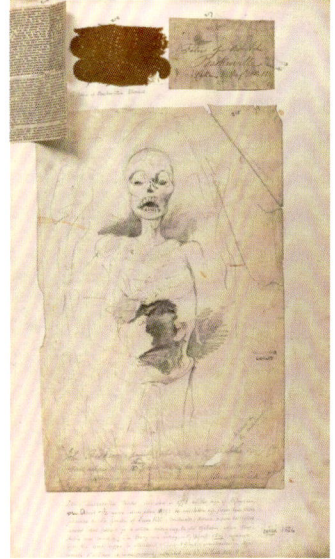

Underwood's sketch of Baskerville's exhumed body.

Anatomy

Baskerville is a serif typeface. The tail of the 'Q' is quite fancy, which some speculate comes from Baskerville's background as a calligrapher.

Typeface designs at the time were still evoking the hand-written word, and the density of the lines in page layouts and appearance of the letterforms is often scribe-like. The basic mechanics of pen calligraphy create the 45-degree stress in characters such as 'b' or 'p' or 'o' that you find in all characters of that time.

By contrast, in Baskerville the stress is not on a slant but rotated to 90 degrees, which is not readily achievable with a pen. A small and subtle shift, but it suggests Baskerville decided to stop replicating the past and to start designing for the technology, which makes a surprisingly big difference to the letterforms.

Baskerville's fancy tail

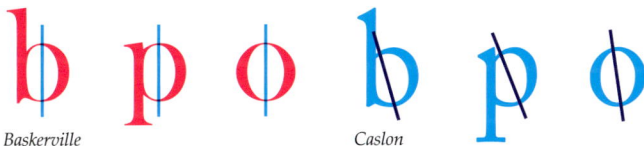

Baskerville   *Caslon*

JNZ

Baskerville

JNZ

Baskerville italic

While the italics match their roman counterparts, there are enough flourishes on the capital 'J' and 'N' or the 'Z' to retain some of the flair of their calligraphic roots.

Baskerville has been in continuous use for 250 years and was one of the five faces available for the first Apple iBook app. The original names of the fonts were based on the sizes: Great Primer, Double Pica Roman Capitals, Brevier Number 1 Roman, Two-line Double Pica Italic Caps. As Simon Garfield points out in *Just My Type*, these sound like a complex coffee order.

It's been said that Baskerville is the reason that 'Transitional' was added to the Vox classification system. Classing a typeface as transitional is a mean-girls move; it is officially 'in between' — not a classic, but not yet modern. Effectively, Baskerville can't sit with the other typefaces. If Baskerville is 'transitional', then it can't be the first 'modern' typeface. We are not the only ones to suspect that John Baskerville's atheism, combined with his being a friend of noted revolutionary Benjamin Franklin, is the real reason Baskerville got dissed by Vox.

What's good, bad and indifferent about Baskerville?

Baskerville is a well-considered, well-proportioned typeface with a well-judged contrast between the thick and thin strokes. The relatively tall x-height means lowercase characters hold their own against the capitals without competing against them.

Another appealing aspect of Baskerville is the clear visual relationship between the roman and the italic faces. Baskerville designed true italics, not a bare minimum sloped version of the roman or an extreme italic found in other typefaces. A side-by-side comparison between the roman and italic of Baskerville would not raise awkward family questions about adoptions (or possible infidelities).

cap height
x-height
baseline

BaSkerVilLe

Lorem ipsum

Baskerville

Lorem ipsum

Baskerville italic

Baskerville

Baskerville in the wild

Compelling research conducted in 2013 by Errol Morris on 45,000 unsuspecting readers in *The New York Times* statistically showed Baskerville to be the most trusted typeface (although it must be said the comparison typefaces did include Comic Sans, along with Helvetica, Trebuchet and Georgia). So if you want people to believe what you say we recommend you set it in Baskerville. This probably explains why a version of Baskerville was used for the wordmark representing the country of Canada.

If Baskerville really is the most trustworthy typeface, should you change your default settings?

Kiss, date, marry or kill?

We think of Baskerville in the same way that we think about Olivia Colman. Colman often plays modest, second-fiddle characters, but once the camera is focused on her something changes. She becomes more complex and fascinating, and surprising qualities start to shine through. She's very British, too (once you've played the queen for two seasons of *The Crown*, if they break you open you probably have the word 'Britannia' running through you like a stick of Brighton rock).

Despite initially being more loved by Europeans, Baskerville is also terribly British, and, just like Olivia Colman, it often plays a supporting role as body copy. Baskerville's interesting complexities are not as immediately noticeable as body copy, but when you look closer the quality shines through. Baskerville is graceful and tasteful. Yes, it's narrow, but in a good way. We would marry Baskerville; it has never been hurtful to our eyes.

(left) The Kate Spade logo reassuringly uses Baskerville to denote quality.

(below) The wordmark for Canada, set in a customized version of Baskerville, says 'trust us, we are Canadian'.

Akzidenz-Grotesk

Designer: Unknown
Date: 1898 (or 1896, depending on who you read)

Akzidenz-Grotesk is a typeface with working-class roots so humble that no designer took credit for it. Originally created for use in invoices, business cards and flyers, whoever made the design decisions for Akzidenz-Grotesk had a clear sense of its purpose: to be useful. As a result, it is self-effacing and honest, made by workers for workers. We count ourselves as proud ex-members of this hi-vis-vest end of graphic design. Join us in a rousing chorus of (design) 'Workers of the World Unite' before you read this chapter.

Akzidenz-Grotesk in a specimen
book from 1912.

abcdefghijklm
nopqrstuvwxyz
ABCDEFGHIJKLM
NOPQRSTUVWXYZ
0123456789!?

abcdefghijklm
nopqrstuvwxyz
ABCDEFGHIJKLM
NOPQRSTUVWXYZ
0123456789!?

Berthold-Plakatschriften

H. Berthold AG
Schriftgießerei und
Messinglinienfabrik
1 Berlin 61
Mehringdamm 43

Zweigwerk Stuttgart
7 Stuttgart-
Bad Cannstatt
Mercedesstraße 9

ERWIN ETTENAUER
Handel mit graph. und papier-
verarbeitenden Maschinen
Wien 1, Rathausplatz 7, Tel. 42 83 86

Akzidenz-Grotesk

A working-class child with no parents

Akzidenz-Grotesk is an early sans serif typeface that was first released around 1898 and is often credited as the main precursor to Helvetica. We don't know precisely who designed Akzidenz-Grotesk. Obviously, someone did, but it requires some detective to find out where this typeface (probably) comes from.

Let's start with the name itself. 'Grotesk' is used in typographic terms to mean sans serif. When used in a non-typographic context, it means bizarre, incongruous or repugnant. It was released by the Berthold Type Foundry of Berlin at a time when there was a preference for blackletter typeforms in Germany, so 'grotesk' was not a flattering way to describe sans serifs, but it gets worse. Sans serifs and slab serif typefaces from the time were sometimes called 'Egyptian', which was the slang term of the time for any new and unusual typefaces. If you are thinking that a bunch of Europeans using 'Egyptian' to describe something being odd, new and different sounds a bit racist, we agree.

Akzidenz comes from the German *akzidenzen*, meaning 'commercial print' — specifically, all print work that isn't books and magazines. In English the closest word we have is 'jobbing', to describe boring work that barely needs a designer — think business cards, invoices, letterheads, ads, the local fast-food-shop flyer — and usually goes straight to a printer to produce. If you have ever worked as an in-house designer at a printer, you know the kind of work Akzidenz-Grotesk was designed for. And this work must be done fast. From personal experience we can tell you that if you spend too much time trying to make this stuff look amazing, you will get fired. Sadly, for all the workers gainfully employed doing this work, there is less and less of it around since design software for non-designers came along.

To sum up, the name Akzidenz-Grotesk means 'jobbing sans'. It's a typeface for people doing an honest day's design work, as in, *'Hans, pass me the Akzidenz-Grotesk, I'll slap together this flyer that the boss wants done right now and I'll meet you down the pub for beers later.'* Not some fancy craft beers, obviously.

(opposite) Akzidenz-Grotesk
specimen, Berthold, 1956.

Ferdinand Theinhardt did not design Akzidenz-Grotesk, but is famous for cutting hieroglyphics – hence this rather fetching portrait, with a background of ancient Egyptian text.

DIE SCHRIFTGIESSEREI FERD. THEINHARDT IN BERLIN WIRD 1908 VON BERTHOLD ERWORBEN

Anfang Januar 1908 wurde auf Betreiben von Dr. Jolles die Schriftgießerei Ferd. Theinhardt in Berlin-Schöneberg angekauft und dann in eine G.m.b.H. umgewandelt. Der Betrieb blieb zunächst noch in Schöneberg, wurde aber im folgenden Jahre nach der Belle-Alliance-Str. 87 in Berlin verlegt. Damit wurde ein alter treuer Kundenkreis, der weit über die Grenzen Berlins hinaus reichte, zu Berthold herübergezogen. Die Kraft dieser Gießerei lag vornehmlich in einem Stamm guter Brotschriften, dann aber in einer Reihe wertvoller orientalischer Schriften, die der Meister THEINHARDT, ein besinnlicher Künstler in seinem Fache, auf Anregung von sprachwissenschaftlichen Forschern oder von Gesellschaften, und in dauernder Verbindung mit ihnen, zur eigenen Freude, zum Teil sogar auch auf eigene Kosten selbst geschnitten hatte. Ein kleines Büchlein, »Lebens-Erinnerungen«, das Theinhardt am Abend seines Lebens nur für einen engeren Freundeskreis geschrieben, gibt darüber fesselnde Erklärungen; es wurde von der Firma Berthold Ende 1920 zum hundertjährigen Gedenken seines Geburts-

Origin story

For about 20 years, type historians thought Akzidenz-Grotesk was designed by Ferdinand Theinhardt, who ran his own type foundry in Berlin in the 19th century, but this has since been disproven. Dutch designer Martin Majoor mounts a compelling argument that Akzidenz-Grotesk is an adaptation of Walbaum and Didot, but we side with Kris Sowersby from the Klim Type Foundry in New Zealand. He points out that Akzidenz-Grotesk may have been derived from Berthold's typeface Schattierte Grotesk, because if you take off its drop shadow you get close to the base style of Akzidenz-Grotesk.

It's likely that the punchcutters at the Berthold Foundry literally chopped off the drop shadow from the matrices for Schattierte Grotesk and just started printing with it. Alternatively, the forerunner of what became the Berthold Type Drawing Office may have done the work. Both places were staffed with teams of women, which means Akzidenz-Grotesk could have been created by a woman, or women, plural.

Schattierte Grotesk with its rather jaunty drop shadow. Squint and we think you can see Akzidenz-Grotesk.

Säntis

(above) Women at work in the Monotype punchcutting room in 1928, the kind of room that Akzidenz-Grotesk may have been designed in (note the male supervisors in suits at the back).

(left) Women in the punchcutting room at Monotype in 1956 checking copper patterns.

The herstory of Type Drawing Offices

Type Drawing Offices created fully functional working typefaces from a designer's drawings or from existing sorts. Teams of workers converted typefaces into the right format for the industrial process used at the time. They made letterforms suitable for hot metal typesetting, then for phototypesetting, and finally for digital production. Born out of the industrial age, Type Drawing Offices experienced their zenith between the 1920s and 1990s, when industrial processes for reproducing type experienced the most change (from hot metal, to photographic, to digital reproduction).

Drawing clerks created the different point sizes, punctuation, accents, bold, italic, expanded and condensed fonts and non-Latin letterforms. Using tools like ruling pens, pantographs and projectors, they would trace and draft multiple versions of the typeface, adjusting and improving as they went along. Drawing clerks weren't type designers but highly skilled drafters, able to pick up and translate the subtleties of a design and make it work within the type foundry constraints.

(above) Annie Burt devising matrix-case arrangements in the Monotype Type Drawing Office in the 1940s.

(right) Woman working in the Berthold Type Drawing Office in the 1980s, preparing a typeface for photographic reproduction.

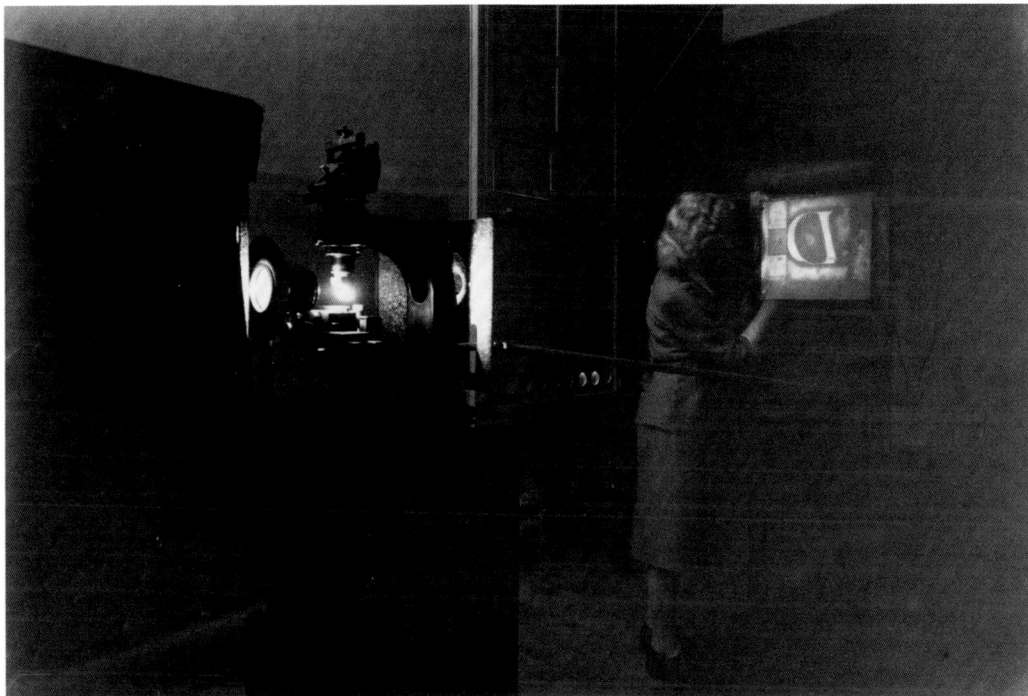

A worker in the Monotype Type Drawing Office uses a projector to trace an old metal sort to create a drawn version of a letter.

It's not clear whether the Berthold Foundry had a Type Drawing Office at the time that Akzidenz-Grotesk was created. Unfortunately, the history of these offices isn't well documented because it was very ordinary industrial work mostly performed by women. Offices were staffed by women because they needed a lot of workers, and women (then, as now) commanded lower wages than men.

Men supervised the teams of women, of course, so any credit for the work of the Type Drawing Office was inevitably attributed to a man. As Virginia Woolf wrote, 'anonymous was a woman', so our completely unsubstantiated theory is that Akzidenz-Grotesk could have been designed by a woman. It's easy to imagine that a woman (or women) on the Berthold Foundry punchcutting factory floor, or a woman working as a drawing clerk, made Akzidenz-Grotesk, but her male supervisor didn't bother (or want) to put his name on such a humble typeface. So, the Berthold Foundry marketing department just slapped a name on the new typeface that described what it was — i.e. 'jobbing sans serif' — and sold Akzidenz-Grotesk without any fanfare.

One person's Grotesque is another person's Egyptian

Akzidenz-Grotesk comes under the Vox classification of a 'Lineal Grotesque'. Grotesque sans serifs are more irregular and awkward than the more refined Neo-Grotesque typefaces like Helvetica.

Just to be confusing, American type designers often called sans serifs 'Gothic' instead of 'Grotesque'. American Gothic typefaces tend to have more open apertures — where a curved stroke almost encloses part of the letter, like the ends of an 's' — than Grotesques. While European Grotesques often feature a curved leg on the capital 'R', there's usually a straight leg on an American Gothic 'R'. Akzidenz-Grotesk has a straight-legged 'R', proving there's always an exception to every type rule.

Akzidenz-Grotesk is a 'monoline' typeface, meaning it has a similar stroke width across all the letters. It has a tall x-height, and the capitals are relatively wide and uniform in width. The stroke endings are less consistently horizontal or vertical than Helvetica. We suspect the digital cuts have been made more uniform, as the metal type versions included variations in x-height, cap height and descender lengths across the family.

After the initial release, Akzidenz-Grotesk was expanded to six styles by 1911, 13 by 1958 and 21 by 1968. There wasn't an Akzidenz-Grotesk italic face until the 1950s, probably because German-speaking/blackletter-using countries relied on a stylistically different typeface for italics rather than a slanted or oblique font.

We have some aesthetic reservations about individual letters of Akzidenz-Grotesk, particularly those closed apertures and the comparative width of the capitals which look a bit... well... clumsy. However, clumsy has its charms.

R R R

Akzidenz-Grotesk   *Franklin Gothic*   *Helvetica*

cap height

x-height

AxedH

baseline

Ge Ge

Akzidenz-Grotesk   *Trade Gothic*

Akzidenz-Grotesk in the wild

Akzidenz-Grotesk was a slow burn and didn't become truly popular until the 1950s and 60s. One of the first things that it was used for was to set the Prussian train timetables, and other not very glamorous uses included making invoice templates. It's somewhat ironic that Akzidenz-Grotesk is now often used for fancy architect studio branding.

The slightly imperfect look of Akzidenz-Grotesk gives it a nice human feel, which might be why the American Red Cross uses it for its branding. Until 2018 it was used for the telltale 'c' that formed the Creative Commons logo. If you are a fan of Dick Bruna's *Miffy* books, you'll see that the publishers used to alternate between typefaces Mercator and Akzidenz-Grotesk.

Donald Trump's 2016 election campaign used Akzidenz-Grotesk Bold Extended for Trump's name on its campaign materials. We don't know if they did this to signal 'working class', but we do know that the designer committed a type crime when they paired it with the only-very-slightly-different sans serif Meta FF for the 'Make America Great Again' bit.

Kiss, date, marry or kill?

A statement headline using a distinctive typeface often needs to be paired with a typeface that will not compete. Akzidenz-Grotesk is a good choice for this kind of supporting role because it is humble and self-effacing.

Akzidenz-Grotesk is one of those actors whose name you can't remember but you recognize in film after film, even though they play vastly different characters. It might never win an Oscar for Leading Actor, but it would surely rack up loads of Best Supporting Actor nominations.

We would date Akzidenz-Grotesk, but it would be a backup to others we would be texting: a typeface to turn to when we are alone on a Saturday night, and a bit bored with the other sans serifs. Which is a shame because, when you think about it, Akzidenz-Grotesk is the ideal partner: confident, supportive, a reassuring presence without needing to show off. It might not be memorable, but Akzidenz-Grotesk is unlikely to irritate you, and it's not hard to work with.

We think we might hit Akzidenz-Grotesk up for a drink sometime. Maybe we just need a few more dates to completely win us over.

(top) An American Red Cross bus.
(above) The old Creative Commons logo.
(right) Display of *Miffy* books.

Mrs Eaves

Designer: Zuzana Licko
Date: 1995

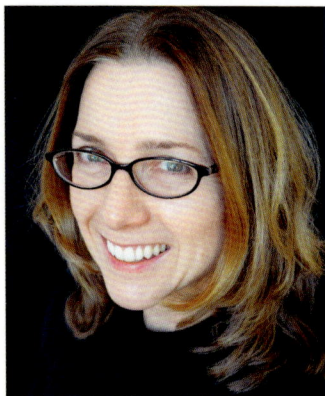

Portrait of Zuzana Licko.

The 1990s were a time during which many type crimes were committed — according to some critics, at least. Typefaces became digital and designers could manipulate, fragment, distort and deconstruct them, igniting the infamous 'legibility wars' in graphic design.

We committed some of these alleged type crimes ourselves as young design students. Sadly, our design teachers thought our work was 'not very good', whereas we still believe it was 'bravely experimental'. We hope that one day they recognize how wrong they were. Just like the critics of type designer Zuzana Licko were forced to when she created the very classically legible Mrs Eaves after years of producing experimental postmodern 'illegible' typefaces.

A woman's work is recognized

Mrs Eaves was designed by Zuzana Licko during the early to mid-1990s, the apex of postmodernism and firmly in the Gen X-era of graphic design. Born in Slovakia in 1961, Licko emigrated to the US with her family in 1968 and studied design at the University of California, Berkeley. She started out in architecture but ended up graduating in 1984 with a degree in Graphic Communications.

Like Steve Jobs before her, Licko became aware of typography while doing a calligraphy class. Unlike Steve Jobs, she did not leave the calligraphy class with a lifelong love of the traditions of type. Left-handed Licko was forced to use her right hand for assignments and her subsequent struggles led her to question tradition.

Licko studied computer programming as part of her degree, and during the summers would help her father, a biomathematician, with data processing. Gen X was the first generation to grow up with computers, giving designers like Licko a comfort level with digital design processes not shared by the old guard. By the time Mrs Eaves came out in 1995 the whole field of graphic design had almost completely transitioned from rubber cement and scalpels to digital production. In the process, many left the profession.

abcdefghijklm
nopqrstuvwxyz
ABCDEFGHIJKLM
NOPQRSTUVWXYZ
0123456789!?

abcdefghijklmnopqrstuvwxyz
ABCDEFGHIJKLM
NOPQRSTUVWXYZ
0123456789!?

FABLE XIX. *The* **Boy** *and the* **Nettle.**

— [SET IN MRS EAVES] —

A little boy playing in the fields,

CHANCED TO BE STUNG BY A

NETTLE

AND CAME CRYING TO HIS FATHER:

❋❋❋❋❋❋❋❋❋❋❋❋❋❋❋❋❋❋❋❋❋❋❋❋❋❋❋❋❋❋❋❋❋

HE TOLD HIM, he had been hurt by that nasty weed
several times before; that he was *always* afraid of it; and
that now he did not but just touch it, as lightly as
possible, when he was so severely stung.

❋❋❋❋❋❋❋❋❋❋❋❋❋❋❋❋❋❋❋❋❋❋❋❋❋❋❋❋❋❋❋❋❋

CHILD SAID HE, your touching it so gently
and timorously is the very *reason* of its hurting you.
A *Nettle* may be handled safely, if you do it with *courage*
and *resolution*: if you seize it *boldly*, and gripe it *fast*,
be assured it will *never* sting you;

❋❋❋❋❋❋❋❋❋❋❋❋❋❋❋❋❋❋❋❋❋❋❋❋❋❋❋❋❋❋❋❋❋

AND YOU WILL MEET MANY SORTS OF

PERSONS

as well as *things* in the world

WHICH OUGHT *to be* TREATED *in the* VERY SAME

MANNER

❖❋❖❋❖❋❋❋❋❖❋❖❋❖

Licko met her husband, Rudy VanderLans, a fellow graphic designer and expat from the Netherlands, while studying at Berkeley. In 1984 they started their own design studio called Emigre (no accents on purpose: it's a designer thing). In the same year, Apple released the first Macintosh and Licko created digital typefaces that embraced the limits of its bitmapp-y technology. The most famous was Lo-Res, which literally blew up the pixelated edges of early digital typefaces to make it a feature of the design.

The history of Mrs Eaves is impossible to separate from the history of *Emigre*, the self-published magazine released by the studio, somewhat erratically, from 1985 to 2005 (no judgement, we know how difficult it is to get a passion project out the door). VanderLans started incorporating Licko's typefaces into the layouts in 1985, giving the magazine a distinctive, new and interesting look that created demand for the typefaces. Emigre started a digital foundry to sell Licko's typefaces, one of the first in the world, and it became the core of their business.

We can't overemphasize the influence of *Emigre* magazine, especially on poor graphic design students whose budgets sadly didn't stretch to the cover price (an exorbitant US$7.95!) Every edition was different and experimental. The magazine brought Jacques Derrida's philosophy of deconstruction into graphic design, doing to type and layouts what Frank Gehry did to buildings. Zuzana Licko and Rudy VanderLans were at the vanguard of postmodernism in graphic design — which brought out the haters.

Shake it off

Emigre was criticized for its illegibility by quite a few famous designers and design commentators. Messiness was anathema to a generation of designers raised on Helvetica and the typographic grid. But, as type designer Tobias Frere-Jones pointed out in his 1994 essay for *Zed Magazine*, if everyone had a computer and could make things precise, why bother doing legible?

Things came to a head in 1991 when Licko said in an interview that blackletter wasn't inherently less readable than roman typefaces, because legibility is just a habit. She argued that the typefaces we find the most legible are only so because we read them the most. After that the 'legibility wars' were off to the races, with the 'grunge' designers set against the modernists. In many ways this was a generational battle, pitting 1950s and 60s designers such as Paul Rand against upstart youngsters like David Carson and April Greiman.

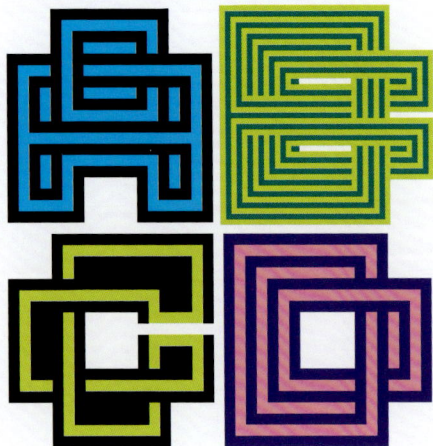

**LO-RES MONOSPACED
DESIGNED BY ZUZANA LICKO**

EMIGRE

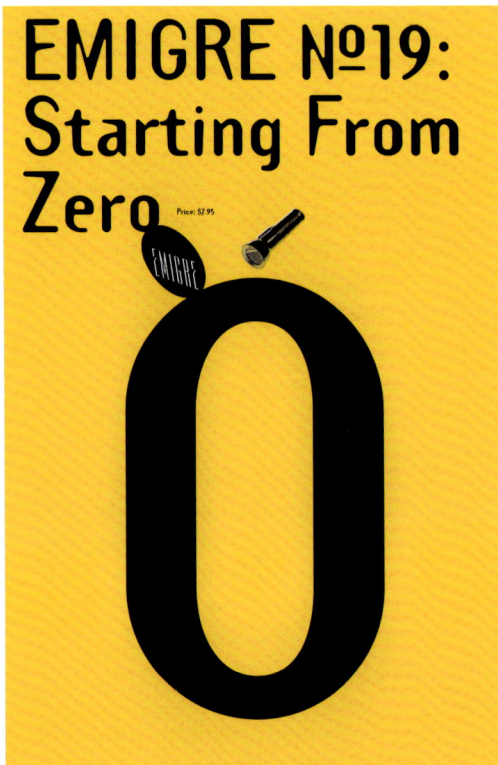

EMIGRE №19:
Starting From
Zero

Lo-Res is one of the most famous of Licko's early experimental digital typefaces. In 2023 Emigre released Lo-Res Monospaced.

An *Emigre* cover from the 1990–94 era of the 'legibility wars'.

The internet was in its infancy, so the fight was carried out through interviews, essays and articles, like design critic Steven Heller's 1993 feature 'Cult of the Ugly' in the influential *Eye Magazine*, and continued in person through cutting exchanges at AIGA (American Institute of Graphic Arts) meetings and design conferences. Legendary designer Massimo Vignelli called *Emigre* garbage and a cultural aberration. Given his propensity for saying negative things to female designers (April Greiman was another target), there's more than a whiff of misogyny about these comments. Mind you, Vignelli never did hold back much, and when he visited our design school in 1992 we thought he was a boring old fart for telling us off for compressing typefaces.

Mrs Eaves was released in 1995, the same year a woman smashed a computer with a sledgehammer on stage at a Seattle design conference as passions raged in the legibility wars (we haven't been able to find out who this was, but we would love to talk sometime). Licko started designing Mrs Eaves in 1992, at the height of hostilities; we can't help wondering if she was thinking, 'Legible? I'll give you legible!'

The legibility wars petered out rather than being 'won', but Zuzana and Rudy definitely won. Once the war was over, the idea that there were 'right ways' to design was gone. In 2016, 11 Emigre typefaces received the ultimate badge of acceptance by being purchased for MoMA's permanent collection in New York.

Zuzana Licko has won many awards, including a 1997 AIGA Gold Medal, which is the equivalent of the lifetime Grammy Award. Despite designing some beautiful and quite traditional typefaces, she is still often described as a radical West Coast type designer. Probably because she never shied away from defending herself.

These days Licko focuses more on fine art, but she continues to design for the Emigre foundry, which now licenses some 600 typefaces. Some of her best-known typefaces include Filosofia, Modula, Base, Citizen, Triplex and Senator.

A loose typeface named after a 'loose woman'

Mrs Eaves is often listed as a classic along with the other heavyweights like Bodoni, Garamond and Baskerville. Which is good because Licko specifically set out to design a classic typeface, just as John Baskerville did, and Mrs Eaves is in fact a revival of Baskerville.

Licko named Mrs Eaves in honour of Sarah Baskerville, who she called one of the forgotten women of type history. If you read the Baskerville chapter you already know Sarah Eaves was John Baskerville's 'housekeeper', then (finally) his wife, who carried on Baskerville's press for 10 years after he died. John Baskerville would have called Sarah Mrs Eaves — at least in public. To this day Sarah Baskerville doesn't get credit for her printing work, and even when her name is printed in very large letters on a title page the book is usually credited to her husband.

Like other type designers making a revival, Licko went back to the original Baskerville printed samples, housed at the University of California, Berkeley library. She noticed that when the lead hit the paper it made the ink spread, so that the characters looked softer and looser on the page than onscreen. So she did the same digitally, shortening the x-height and thickening the contrasty-ness, making the thickness of the strokes more even overall. The result is that Mrs Eaves has less contrast than Baskerville, but retains its openness.

Licko's design choices make Mrs Eaves thicker, softer looking, rounder, more vertically compressed, and really quite different to Baskerville. We think of Mrs Eaves as more of a homage than a straight revival, which is very postmodern and on-brand for Zuzana Licko.

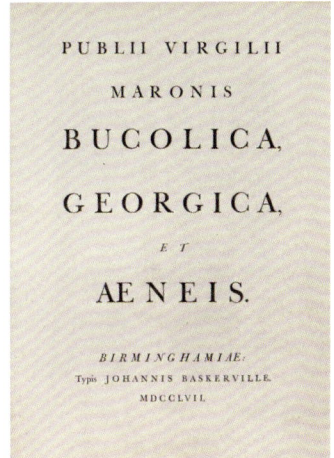

PUBLII VIRGILII

MARONIS

BUCOLICA,

GEORGICA,

ET

AENEIS.

BIRMINGHAMIAE:
Typis JOHANNIS BASKERVILLE.
MDCCLVII.

(top) No known portraits of Sarah Baskerville exist, but we like to think that this is her with her daughter in front of Easy Hill, Baskerville's mansion outside Birmingham.

(above) A copy of Baskerville's *Publii Virgilii Maronis. Bucolica, Georgica, et Aeneis,* which Licko consulted to make her revival typeface, is still available to check out of the special collection at the UC Berkeley library.

Mrs Eaves
A typeface designed
by Zuzana Licko.
Introducing
Mrs Eaves XL Regular
and XL Narrow.
Licensed and
distributed by
Emigre.

There is a certain
that it was
HIS TALENTS *of* RIDICULE
ut pleaded excuse for
much the rather
N NEW YORK C
y that nasty weed
ndeterminately
AID THE SPANI
riend smiled at her apprehensions
hands *of an* informer
TIMOROUSLY IS THE VERY REASON

A later 'XL' version of Mrs Eaves was made with a higher x-height just for body copy.

Mrs Eaves was originally designed as a display serif typeface for headlines and small blurbs of text, not for body copy. Its low x-height means Mrs Eaves needs to be set larger for body copy, and it needs loose letterspacing to read well. You can set the original version as body text, but really, why would you?

A lovely set of ligatures

As a revival of Baskerville, Mrs Eaves is classified the same way: 'Transitional' in the Vox classification system. It comes in all the things: italic, roman, bold and bold italic. We would argue that Mrs Eaves has the best sets of small caps in the business. Small caps allow you to mimic upper- and lowercase text but in all caps, and there are plenty to choose from, including Petite Caps, Basic Small Caps and All Small Caps.

Mrs Eaves has lovely old-style (or non-lining) numerals, where parts of the numbers sit either below the baseline or protrude above the x-height. But it also comes in lining caps, which are optically aligned top and bottom to the cap height and baseline. Think of them as the shaping underwear of typography — no unsightly bumps, so you can make smooth flush edges with your numbers.

Mrs Eaves has a wonderful set of ligatures. A ligature comes from the Latin 'to bind' and is a combination of two letters into one form, where they would otherwise crash into each other if they were set together. Think of two 'f's in a row, or 'f' and 'l', or 's' and 't'. The letters are physically joined together so they are spaced perfectly. Ligatures are both functional and decorative. The Mrs Eaves ligatures look fancy, as befits a typeface designed for display.

Because it needs looser tracking some designers argue that you should just use Baskerville instead. Indeed, British design critic Robin Kinross said the need for loose spacing limits its use. We note that Kinross said this while he was handing Licko a 1999 design award for Mrs Eaves. Rude.

Lorem ipsum

Baskerville

Lorem ipsum

Mrs Eaves

LOREM IPSUM

petite caps

LOREM IPSUM

small caps

fi fl sp st gi ct

decorative ligatures

Mrs Eaves in the wild

Mrs Eaves is one of the best-selling typefaces from the last 25 years, so you will see it in lots of places. With stunning small caps and a lovely italic, you'll find it used wherever a designer wants a stately but approachable classic look. This makes Mrs Eaves a good choice for wine labels, wedding invitations and book covers — especially poetry and historical literary fiction. Which is probably why Penguin uses Mrs Eaves for its Pocket Classics series alongside Futura.

Which brings us to the question, if it needs to be set so loosely, should Mrs Eaves be your default typeface?

Kiss, date, marry or kill?

Mrs Eaves can be polarizing because of the letterspacing, but mostly because it has been overused. We agree that spaced-out Mrs Eaves is a visual cliché, especially on serious poetry books, but we love it and have done since 1995.

We intend to stay married to Mrs Eaves. The small caps especially are lovely. We think of Mrs Eaves as being like Emma Thompson: intelligent, beautiful, classic and versatile. We never get sick of watching her act, or of seeing Mrs Eaves, even after all these years.

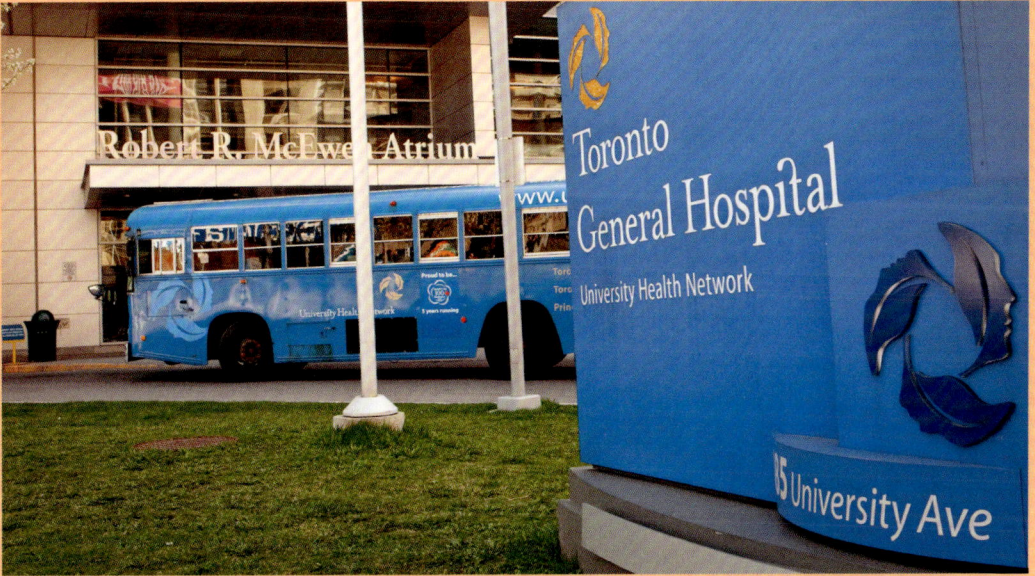

(above) Mrs Eaves is versatile too. The Toronto General Hospital system uses it to give the hospital a reassuringly classic look, while maintaining a 'modern medical practice happens here' kind of feel.

(left) Mrs Eaves inline is decorative and pairs well with classic Mrs Eaves italic on this wine label set for Château des Arras (design by Martin Lavielle and Eléonore Ampuy).

(opposite) The Penguin Pocket Classics covers team up two classic typefaces, Mrs Eaves and Futura.

TRAJAN

Designer: Carol Twombly
Date: 1989

Portrait of Carol Twombly at work; ironically, not on a computer.

Trajan was designed by Carol Twombly and released in 1989 — just in time for us to enthusiastically overuse it as design students. The monument that inspired Trajan was erected almost 1,900 years ago, and we are going to start with the man who put it there, Emperor Trajan (Marcus Ulpius Traianus to his friends), for good reasons. Promise.

Trajan was Roman Emperor from 98 to 117 CE. He famously commemorated 'his' triumph in the Dacian Wars with a victory column — 35 metres (115 feet) tall including the pedestal — and constructed as a vertical stack of Carrara marble drums. His victory in Dacia enriched the Empire with several valuable goldmines, so it doesn't sound like money was an object.

Today the column is very plain white marble, Roman Empire-y looking, but like all classical architecture and statues it used to be painted rather garishly, which helps you understand the thing better as a piece of propaganda, which it totally was. Unlike some of his more unsavoury predecessors, contemporary ancient sources are unanimously positive about Trajan. Even one thousand years later he got a good rap in Dante's *Divine Comedy*, proving once again propaganda pays off.

Or maybe it was the typography. The inscription carved at the base of the column is the most famous example of Roman square capitals (*capitalis monumentalis*). Characterized by sharp, straight lines, supple curves, thick and thin strokes, angled stresses and incised serifs this typeface was designed to be read from below. The bottom letters are smaller than those at the top to allow for perspective. Those Romans really thought of everything.

ABCDEFGHIJKL
MNOPQRSTU
VWXYZ
0123456789!?

ABCDEFGHIJKL
MNOPQRSTU
VWXYZ
0123456789!?

Trajan

The perils of stonemasonry and the origins of signwriting

No matter how much Dacian gold you have to burn through in your budget, inscribing stone is an expensive and tricky enterprise. After quarrying, dressing and transporting the stone, if the letters were then badly proportioned or poorly executed, a lot of money would have been wasted. At this point the stone-cutter would be in serious trouble. Which, set in the context of the Roman Empire, sounds ominous. So ancient typographers needed a solid drafting process to ensure they did good work.

One theory is that Roman square capital letterforms are a result of this stone-cutters' problem (of wanting to stay alive), and owe their character to the use of a brush to paint them onto the surface of the marble prior to carving. The wide edge of a brush held more or less parallel to the ground would produce a broad stroke when moved horizontally and a thin stroke when moved vertically.

Edward Catich, who inspired Twombly when she was designing Trajan, had an alternative theory. Catich was an American Roman Catholic priest, teacher and calligrapher who made the study of Trajan's Column his life's work. He apparently enjoyed touring in bands as well, so sounds rather hip for a priest. Catich speculated that reed pens were the reason for the thick and thin strokes of the letterforms, and for the serifs: the top serif from a movement of the pen to get the ink flowing, the bottom serif from a finishing flick, because the calligraphers wanted to balance these marks out with similar ones on the opposite side of the main stroke.

As a signwriter himself, Catich had practical experience with the same tools Roman artisans used, so he knew what he was talking about. He once wrote that as a modern-day signwriter he would have been able to become a journeyman in Trajan's Rome.

Carol Twombly had hand skills too, but she came from a different time, when type designers' tools had become digital.

A woman can appropriate the work of a man, for a change

Carol Twombly was fascinated by calligraphy and palaeography (the study of historic writing systems and dating and deciphering old manuscripts), hence her interest in Catich's work. Trajan was launched as one of a trio of typefaces marketed as 'Modern Ancients', the other two being Lithos and Charlemagne, and they work together as a sort of typographic bridge spanning ancient Greek through Roman to medieval styles.

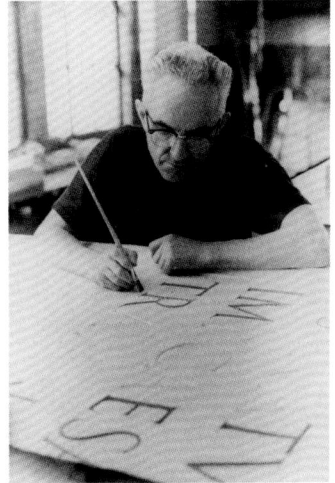

(above) Edward Catich demonstrating how to write *capitalis monumentalis*.

(opposite) View of the inscription on the pedestal of Trajan's Column in Rome. The message is surprisingly mundane: basically a boast about how much dirt was excavated to make way for the column.

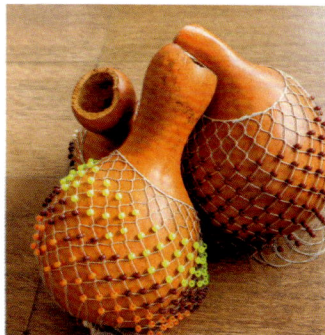

Intricate beading on West African *shekeres*. Still finicky, but a more fun sort of finicky.

Twombly was born in 1959 in Concord, Massachusetts, in the US, and initially studied sculpture at the Rhode Island School of Design before switching her major to graphic design. After graduating, she worked for a year in a Boston design studio before accepting an invitation to join the new Digital Typography programme at Stanford University. Twombly was one of only five students to graduate with a MSc. in computer science and graphic design from this short-lived course. When she left Stanford in the late 1980s she joined Adobe Systems as a type designer.

Among the prestigious recognition for her work, Twombly received the inaugural Morisawa Gold Prize in 1984, and this was her very first entry into an international type-design competition. In 1994 she was presented the Prix Charles Peignot for 'Promising Typeface Designer Under 35' by the Association Typographique Internationale, the first woman to be awarded this title and only the second American.

In 1999, at what many would consider the height of her career, Twombly left it all behind. She quit Adobe, and quit making typefaces.

These boots were made for walking

Biographer Nancy Stock-Allen claims that Twombly became increasingly uncomfortable with all the attention at conferences, about Adobe marketing materials and her role in the company in general. In 2014 Twombly herself cited her own decreasing interest in designing fonts for onscreen display, as well as the specific market failure of Adobe's 'multiple master technology' — which was supposed to be a game-changer in the manipulation of digital type but never really took off.

Twombly seems much happier now as an independent artist, textile painter and decorator of baskets and *shekeres* (a West African percussion instrument consisting of a gourd covered with beaded netting). We might consider this a 'reverse John Baskerville', using her typeface design to fund her artistic endeavours. We get it. Making typefaces is probably not as fun digitally as it used to be manually. Plus you have to really focus on the tiniest of finicky details that pretty much no one will ever notice. It would be enough to drive any designer to consider other career options.

Anatomy

As a serif, the Vox classification of Trajan is an 'Incised Glyphic'. It's also known as a display face because, in keeping with its classical origins, it features only capitals, with no lowercase letterforms (although a later version released by Adobe includes small caps). This does place some limits on its usability, however, and we don't recommend anyone try to set body copy with this typeface.

Other type designers have been inspired by Roman square capitals over the years, including Frederic Goudy. One subtle but noticeable change Carol Twombly made between her typeface and the original inscriptions is the slight flattening of the bowl of the 'D' and curve of the 'C' to create a more even cap height and baseline. Overall the serifs are more pronounced as well.

The result is one of the most elegant, proportionally pleasing typefaces around. It is sharp and lean in all the right places, combined with smooth curves and enough contrast in the stroke and the widths of individual characters to create a pleasing visual rhythm when reading the text. In her design, Twombly successfully references history without looking like pastiche.

Twombly's Trajan typeface compared to the letterforms on the Roman column.

Trajan in the wild

If you think that Twombly turning her back on her success is controversial, try typing 'Trajan' into a search engine and see how many links you get demanding that you NEVER use this typeface if you ever want to be respected as a designer. Which is deeply unfair. Mind you, if you are basing your design choices on the advice of random websites with titles like 'Top 7 Fonts Designers Despise' and 'The 8 Worst Fonts in the World', then you've probably already lost the battle for credibility as a designer.

It is too simplistic to condemn Trajan as the font of choice for lazy designers. However, bundling it up in a font suitcase for anyone who had access to Adobe software products at a time when digital publishing was really taking off was clearly a mixed blessing. Trajan is an undeniably polished and elegant typeface and people want to associate their product or layout with that sophistication and attractiveness. So it is only a short step down to using (abusing?) the elegance and polish of Trajan to upsell a less-than-quality product or message.

As you might expect, Hollywood has taken to this in a big way. There's a short but entertaining YouTube video, *How One Typeface Took Over Movie Posters*, which describes the industry's addiction to Trajan, and in particular looks at the work of Belgium graphic designer Yves Peters, a movie poster aficionado. He laments the demise of the old individual hand lettering of Hollywood posters and the rise of more generic digital designs. In surveying some 15,000 film posters he noticed a rapid and lasting trend in the use of Trajan after it debuted in 1992 for the movie *At Play in the Fields of the Lord*, eventually becoming, as Yves suggests, the Arial of movie posters.

Or, to paraphrase filmmaker Kirby Ferguson in his YouTube take on the same topic, Trajan starts out conveying 'Roman Epic Movie', then the 'Roman' part fades away, then the word 'Epic, leaving just the word 'Movie'.

Trajan is (over) used for Christian design projects too, especially church logos. It probably feels biblical, but with more gravitas than Lithos or — God forbid — Papyrus. Less 'TV evangelist' and more 'non-threatening contemporary Christian'. It's no accident that it was the typeface chosen for the Mitt Romney (US senator and famous Mormon) 2012 presidential campaign.

Kiss, date, marry or kill?

If ever there was a strong case for a mercy killing, it would be Trajan. It's not inherently bad, it's just that bad things have been done in its name; but that's not entirely its fault. Maybe if we laid Trajan to rest for a while, and everyone from Hollywood to wedding invite designers took a break from it, we could resurrect this typeface for future enjoyment.

A less extreme alternative might be to encourage the use of Trajan as a secondary typeface, as it pairs surprisingly well with some pretty outré display typefaces. Treat it like the quiet friend that we bring when we hang out with a loud friend and we need a buffer.

What we are certain of is that the very fine work of Carol Twombly should be viewed on its own merits, and not through the lens of other people's inappropriate design choices. Maybe then the dismissive 'world's worst' tag will fade away from those blog post titles, leaving just the 'fonts to use' bit, and we can all get back to admiring Trajan.

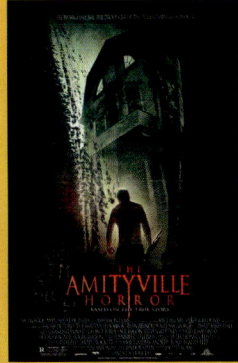

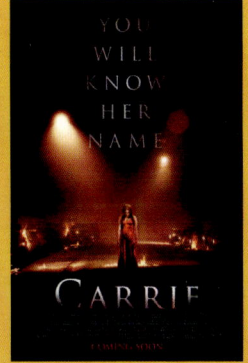

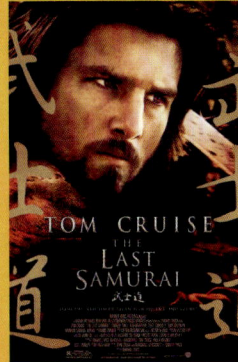

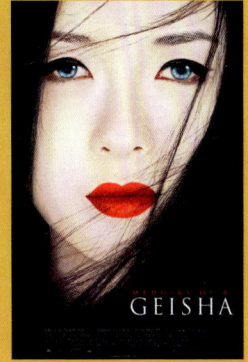

(above) Trajan has been embraced by
B-grade, horror and big Hollywood movies.
At Play in the Fields of the Lord (1991), the
movie poster that apparently started it all,
and some other notable movies that have
used Trajan: *The Amityville Horror* (2005),
Carrie (2013), *The Last Samurai* (2003) and
Memoirs of a Geisha (2005).

(right) Trajan being used in the 2012
Romney/Ryan presidential campaign.

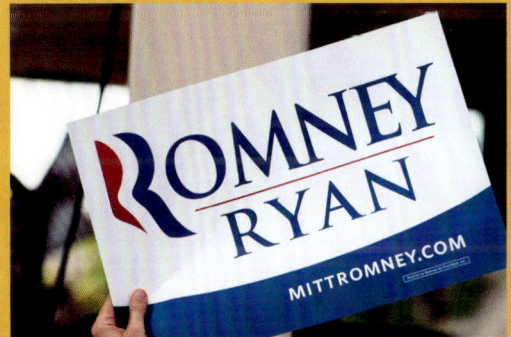

Novarese

Designer: Aldo Novarese
Date: 1978

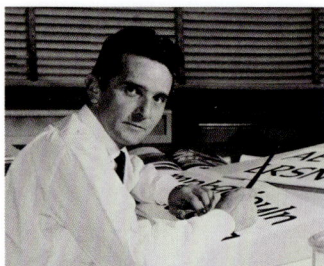

Well, hello there Aldo Novarese.

We will always disagree about Novarese but have resolved to be amicable about our differences. This compromise was facilitated by a cocktail called the *Aperitivo del Tipografo*, which we choose to translate as 'the Typographer's Tipple'. It's a 50/50 mix of mineral water and Carpano Punt e Mes Vermouth. This tastes exactly as you would expect: strong.

If you have those ingredients to hand, why not pour yourself a glass, kick back, and enjoy a little Italian aperitif? It just happens to come from Turin, the same place as Aldo Novarese — easily the best-looking typeface designer in this book.

A handsome typeface from a handsome man

Born in 1920, Aldo Novarese left Pontestura, his hometown in the north of Italy, for the city of Turin at the tender age of 10. Young Aldo was enrolled at the Scuola Artieri Stampatori (School of Printing Crafts), then spent three years at the specialist typography school Scuola di Tipografica Giuseppe Vigliardi Paravia. Meaning that Novarese spent high school learning how to engrave, print and make typefaces instead of failing maths classes like we did.

In 1936 Novarese became an apprentice draughtsman for Nebiolo, Italy's *primo* type foundry. However, his design career was interrupted by the outbreak of World War II, when the foundry was redirected to make airplane and bomb parts. The Nebiolo Foundry was subsequently bombed by the Allies. Sadly, this destroyed their archives, which had dated back to their founding in 1878.

abcdefghijklm

nopqrstuvwxyz

ABCDEFGHIJKLM

NOPQRSTUVWXYZ

0123456789!?

abcdefghijklm

nopqrstuvwxyz

ABCDEFGHIJKLM

NOPQRSTUVWXYZ

0123456789!?

(right) The Nebiolo Foundry in Turin in better times.

(below) Microgramma is a great 'sci-fi'-looking typeface, a severe, squarish sans serif that's perfect for a job like designing space habitat signage.

It wasn't just the trouble at the Nebiolo Foundry that stalled Novarese's career. He was imprisoned in 1939 for refusing military service and protesting Italy's involvement in the war, and only avoided hard labour thanks to the gold medal he won in the 1938 Ludo Juveniles art competition. Given the competition was a 'celebration of fascist culture', we can only imagine the award ceremony was awkward for him.

Novarese didn't sit out the war entirely though. He joined the partisan resistance against the German invaders, was shot, and only managed to survive by hiding under the bodies of his dead comrades.

After the war Novarese returned to the Nebiolo foundry, which was allowed to make typefaces again, and in 1952 was appointed director of the design studio. That same year, he won a gold medal at the Milan Trade Fair for his typefaces. By then this included Microgramma, which he worked on with his boss Alessandro Butti. Microgramma is the precursor to Novarese's even more famous typeface, Eurostile.

Despite the success of the design studio under Novarese's directorship, the foundry struggled in the post-war Italian economy. It failed to transition to phototype technology in the 1960s. Novarese left in 1972, and in 1978 the foundry declared bankruptcy. Novarese worked for a couple of years as a consultant for Reber R4, Italy's answer to Letraset, before settling into freelance type design work for the rest of his career.

Novarese wrote two books: *Alfa-Beta: The Study and Design of Type* in 1964, and *Il Segno Alfabetico* (*Alphabet Signs*) in 1971. A titan of Italian type design, he designed more than 70 typefaces (200 if you include all the different weights). Even if some of his typefaces are very silly (looking at you, Estro), and some are, as the Italians would (and did) say, *troppo profumato* (too fancy) — take a bow Stop and Ritmo. Today the aesthetic looks a little quaint or even humorously deluded, but you can understand the appeal of this techno-optimism of the space race for someone like Aldo Novarese, who lived through the horror of continental conflict and the flux of the post-war period. But Novarese did also design the solid classics Nova Augustea, Fontanesi and Novarese.

Aldo Novarese died in Turin, just after finishing his very last typeface design, in 1995.

International (type classification system) encounters

Novarese was a good friend of Maximilien Vox, creator of the Vox classification system. Maximilien Vox was actually a pseudonym for Samuel Monod, who came from a very conservative family who didn't approve of his career as an artist, political cartoonist and journalist, hence the fake name.

In 1950 Vox had the idea of bringing together his friends and colleagues — typographers, editors, photographers and other creatives — to 'reflect on their industries' at a summer retreat called Les Rencontres

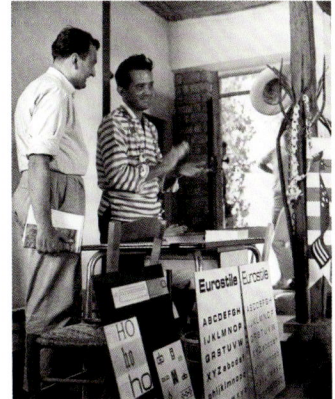

(top) The later Eurostile is basically the same typeface as Microgamma, but with a lowercase. Here it's used in signage for Washington Dulles International Airport.

(above) Aldo Novarese presenting at Les Rencontres Internationales de Lure in the 1950s.

(right) Novarese in his office at the back of the Nebiolo studio in the 1960s. Promotional materials for some of his typefaces can be seen on the wall.

(below) Stop, from 1971, is another sci-fi-looking typeface, demonstrating Novarese's knack for picking up on the zeitgeist and turning it into a typeface.

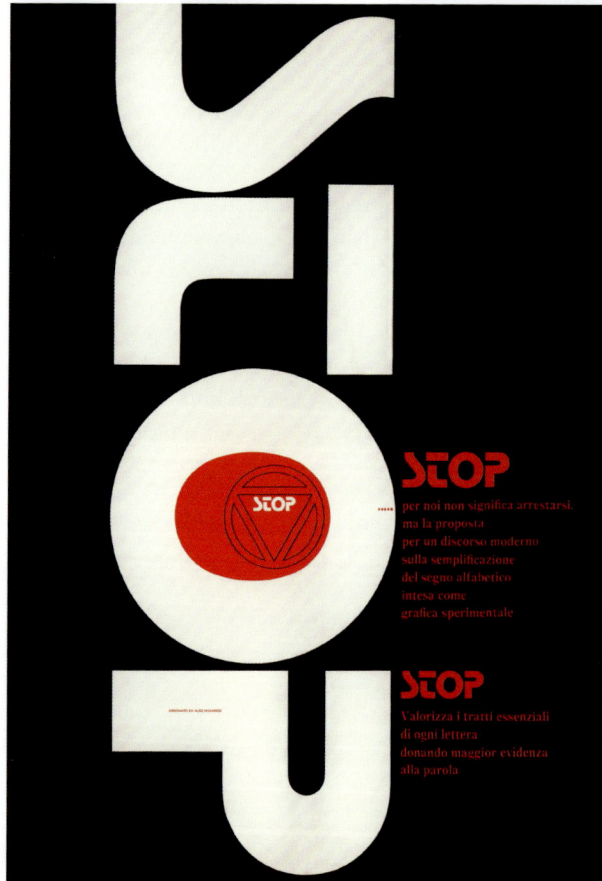

STOP
per noi non significa arrestarsi,
ma la proposta
per un discorso moderno
sulla semplificazione
del segno alfabetico
intesa come
grafica sperimentale

STOP
Valorizza i tratti essenziali
di ogni lettera
donando maggior evidenza
alla parola

Internationales de Lure (International Encounters in the town of Lure). Constituted as an Association in 1957 the Compagnons de Lure still meet in the last week of August, staying at La Chancellerie, a building in the village donated by Vox for the purpose.

The website claims there are workshops and presentations, but to us it sounds like San Francisco's Bohemian Club meetings, but for type nerds. Similarly, they hung about in forest groves, indulging in plays with masks and some dubious evening ceremonies. At the meetings, the 'Chancellor of Lurs' would drink the *coup de bleu* (water mixed with methylene) while facing the lake at sunset. The companions subscribed to an oath composed by Vox in 1953:

> *By the incarnate verb, by Alpha and Omega, by the mountain of Lure, I vow to despise the lucre, to renounce the gloriole, and to serve the spirit.*

There's still *coup de bleu*, although they call it afternoon drinks now. We don't know if anyone takes the oath any more, but it all seems like a mysterious secret society for designers, and we would very much like to be invited to the next one.

Novarese and Vox came up with rival classification systems within a couple of years of each other. Vox created his type classification system in 1954 and Novarese his around 1956/57. Vox's was widely adopted in 1967, so there may have been some awkward silences at Les Rencontres Internationales after that. Novarese's system is composed of 10 categories: Renaissance Antiqua, Baroque Antiqua, Classic Antique, Scrif Stressed Linear Antique, Serifless Linear, Antique Variants Scripts and Handwritten/Broken Scripts, with subcategories underneath.

The Compagnons de Lure in the 1950s with Vox at the front.

A strange italic

Novarese is a serif, and under its creator's system fits into the Egizi or Egyptian category, a subcategory of Serif Stressed Linear Antique. In Vox classification, it is considered a 'Glyphic'. It has a low stroke contrast, a vertical axis on the curved strokes and flaring serifs that imitate carved inscriptions. But type classification is not a precise art, and Novarese shares some characteristics with a subcategory of Mechanistic typefaces known as Clarendons or Ionics. These include bracketed serifs, a low stroke contrast and a relatively tall x-height combined with shorter ascenders and descenders.

Novarese has all the best things you associate with Italian design. It has the gravitas of a serif without feeling too staid or dated. The typeface comes in four weights: we are not big fans of the bolder faces, but the roman is elegant and beautifully proportioned. Some people think the 'Q' is ridiculous, the serifs wimpy, the counters too round and the uppercase 'P' too droopy. But not us.

The other key (some would say odd) feature is the italic face, which is more upright than most and much narrower than the roman characters. You could almost be forgiven for thinking they're two different typefaces because only the lowercase characters in this font are italicized. This may look like Aldo had one too many Typographer's Tipples; Novarese would have argued that back when italics were first designed, printers would set the first letter of a line of poetry in roman and the rest in italics, so his choice is historically accurate. However, when people defend their choices by claiming historical accuracy, sometimes you're left thinking, yeah, not sure authenticity is the problem here. It just looks strange.

Lorem ipsum

low stroke modulation, flared serifs, vertical axis

cap height
x-height

Abghijps

baseline

Est Per Quam

Novarese

Novarese in the wild

Thanks to the roman and italic fonts, with Novarese you get two very different character sets for the price of one. Novarese pairs nicely with sans serifs, as these often share a relatively tall x-height. You'll find Novarese used in books, usually on the cover.

The highest profile usage of Novarese is the branding for football's UEFA Champions League, which incorporates the bold font in its logo. Fans of the musician Paul Simon would also recognize the roman uppercase from the cover artwork of the 1986 album, *Graceland*. The jeweller Swarovski uses an adapted version, and haters suggest that they have actually achieved the impossible and made Novarese worse.

Kiss, date, marry or kill?

Who better to compare this typeface to than the Italian national treasure Sophia Loren: beautiful, stylish and full of contradictions: a staunch Roman Catholic whose marriage was initially bigamous; a sex symbol who put her career on hold to care for her children; a Hollywood star who became a jailbird (although she was cleared of those tax evasion charges). Sophia has aged well, and so has Novarese. Created in 1978, it is now middle-aged but still looks damn fine on the page.

One of us has stayed faithful to Novarese for years. Like most old married couples, it means putting up with, or working around, some aspects of Novarese because of what else it brings to the relationship: reliability, familiarity and trust.

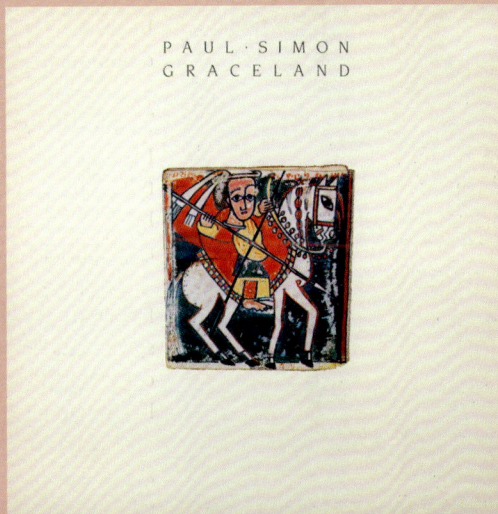

(above) A customized version of Novarese used in signage for Swarovski; all caps used on the *Graceland* album cover.

(right) International football's governing body UEFA chose Novarese for their competition branding.

Bell Centennial

Designer: Matthew Carter
Date: 1978

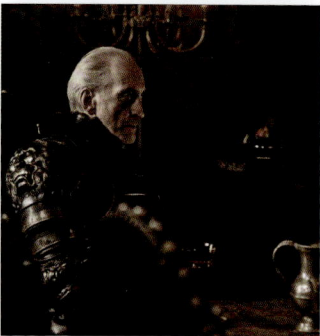

Matthew Carter, and Tywin Lannister from TV's *Game of Thrones*. Separated at birth?

We think there is an uncanny resemblance between famed typeface designer Matthew Carter and *Game of Thrones*'s Tywin Lannister. But this is not why he has been called a villain to his face by fans of Futura. They resent him for designing the web typeface Verdana, which replaced Futura as IKEA's corporate typeface in 2011.

Matthew Carter's long career spans physical, photosetting and digital type technologies, and it was thanks to this immersion in the craft that he was able to solve the technical issues that plagued the production of a once vital household item: the telephone directory.

Type in the blood

Instead of the famed Casterly Rock gold, Carter's inheritance was typography. His father was Harry Carter, a book designer and print historian at Oxford University Press. Carter senior was a friend, archivist and assistant to Stanley Morison, designer of Times New Roman.

Matthew was born in London in 1937, the same year that his father and Morison began cataloguing all of the known pre-1800 type specimens. Young Matthew seems to have been interested in type very early on. His mother, who prepared scale architectural drawings for a living, cut a set of vinyl letters for him to play with as a young child.

Thanks to Harry's connections, Carter secured a year-long internship at Royal Joh Enschedé at the age of 19. This prestigious printing company still operates out of Haarlem in the Netherlands and specializes in security documents, stamps and banknotes. While there he studied punchcutting under P.H. Rädisch, making him one of the last people in Europe to be formally trained in this industry as a living practice, although it was almost obsolete even at the time he was learning.

Bell Centennial

abcdefghijklm
nopqrstuvwxyz
ABCDEFGHIJKLM
NOPQRSTUVWXYZ
0123456789!?

ABCDEFGHIJKLM
NOPQRSTUVWXYZ
ABCDEFGHIJKLM
NOPQRSTUVWXYZ
0123456789!?

(right) *Private Eye* still uses Carter's design for its masthead.

(below) Matthew Carter sees his work all the time whenever he's on campus at Yale.

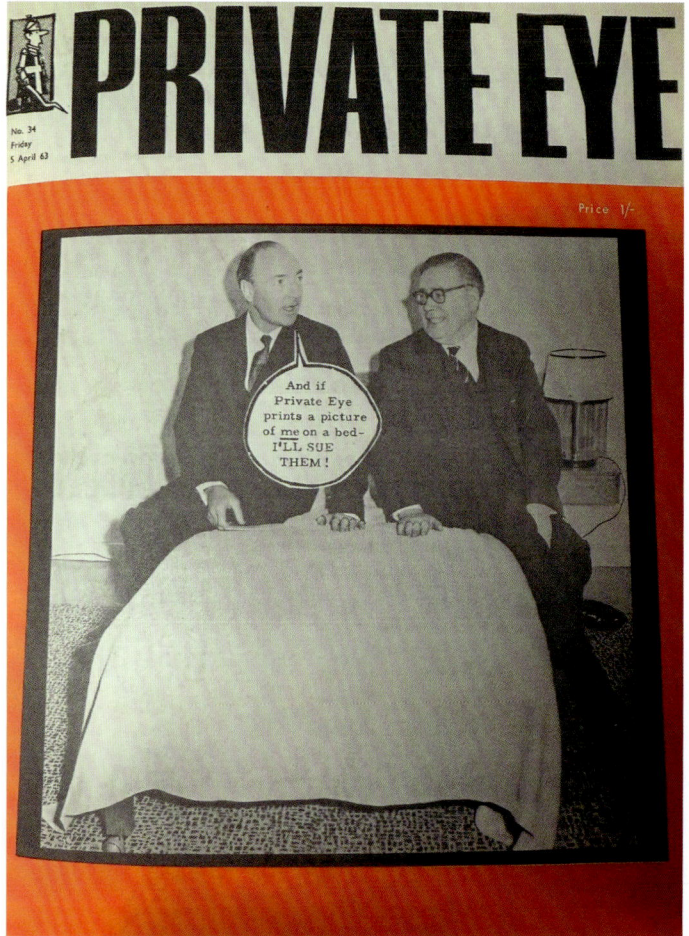

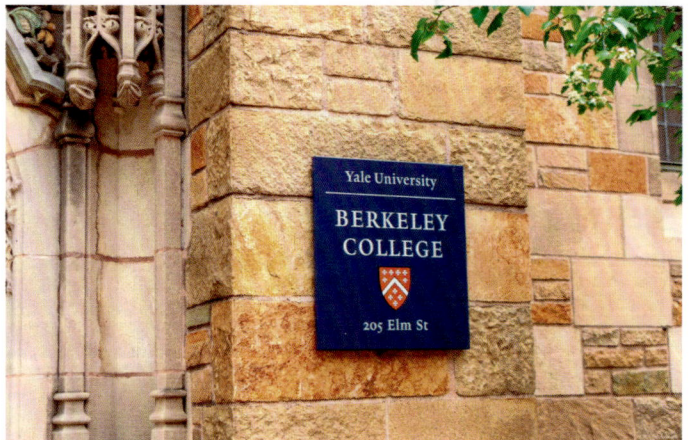

Bell Centennial

If you read about punchcutting in the introduction to this book, you will have an appreciation of the kind of skill Carter possesses. He has spoken about how his experience forced him to think very hard before committing to a design, because he had one chance to get it right, and if he missed he would destroy days of work.

Carter returned to London in the early 1960s to work as a freelance type and graphic designer. During this time he cut a semi-bold version of Dante (a classic book-printing typeface) for the Monotype Corporation and designed the masthead for *Private Eye* magazine.

Carter has always been on the edge of technology and type. In 1963 he was appointed typographic advisor to Crosfield Electronics, the British distributors of Photon phototypesetting machines. But by 1965 Carter had left the UK to design typefaces for Mergenthaler Linotype in the US, one of the two leading manufacturers of book and newspaper typesetting equipment. Mergenthaler Linotype's typesetting equipment had by then expanded from hot metal machines to include laser typesetters, scanners and typesetting computers.

Crossing the pond

Carter visited New York in the mid-1960s and talks about the time he spent there, visiting the studios of celebrated graphic designers Milton Glaser and Herb Lubalin, as life-changing. Seeing what other designers were doing with type shocked him out of what he called his 'typographic privilege' in the then quite conservative London design scene. This trip also put him on a path to moving to the US, which is how he began working at Linotype.

Carter has taught in Yale University's graphic design programme since 1976. He designed the university's corporate typeface (imaginatively named Yale), for which he focused more on the uppercase than the lowercase characters as he knew the building signage would be set in capitals.

In 1981 Carter was appointed Royal Designer for Industry in the UK, which is the highest accolade for British designers. In that same year he founded the type foundry Bitstream Inc. in Marlborough, Massachusetts, with fellow expat Mike Parker.

Parker had been director of Mergenthaler Linotype and was instrumental in making available their library of 1000+ typefaces wherever Linotype equipment was in use. As a result the library became the industry standard. But by 1981 sales of typesetting equipment were dwindling and the use of personal computers was expanding. Carter and Parker saw the opportunity to monetize the typefaces themselves through licensing for digital design and production.

Bitstream was a commercial success but was not without controversy. It was criticized for offering cheap digital versions of pre-existing typefaces that it hadn't actually designed. Although this was not technically illegal, fellow type designer John Hudson denounced it as one of the worst cases of piracy in the history of type — the sort of thing you could never get away with today.

Carter left Bitstream Inc. in 1991, and the following year founded Carter & Cone Type Inc., a digital type foundry, with Cherie Cone. She was a founding member of Bitstream Inc., and another ex-Mergenthaler staffer. Cone runs the business side of the partnership, which is still going. They have produced custom typefaces for MoMA, *The Washington Post*, *The New York Times* and Microsoft, among many others.

The list of typefaces designed by Carter is long and includes Big Caslon, Cochin and Snell Roundhand. Carter was one of the first to design typefaces just for the web. In fact, he is perhaps best known for designing the web typefaces Georgia, Tahoma and Verdana. For a long time these were the only true web fonts available, which caused web designers to become very bored and consequently annoyed with Matthew Carter (another reason he has been unfairly regarded as a type villain).

Matthew Carter has collected a multitude of accolades over the course of a long and stellar career, including the Goudy Award for Outstanding Contribution to the Printing Industry, the Chrysler Award for Innovation in Design, a Lifetime Achievement Award at the US National Design Awards (for which he was invited to the White House) and a Commander of the Order of the British Empire (CBE) for services to typography and design. If there was a real-life design equivalent of the Hand of the King, he probably would have nabbed that as well.

Happy anniversary, I designed you a typeface

In 1975 the American Telephone and Telegraph Company (AT&T), through Mike Parker, commissioned Carter to design a replacement for their telephone directory typeface, Bell Gothic. At the time the Bell company still had control of the whole US telephone system and was celebrating 100 years of business, hence: Bell Centennial. (Although can we just say it's not that hard to stay in business that long when you have such a huge monopoly.)

When was the last time you bothered to memorize even an important telephone number? We hold vast telecom directories in the palms of our hands these days, and can quickly find any number, personal or commercial, local and international. But it wasn't always this easy. We forget (or have never experienced) how much the printed version of the directory used to be an important part of the fabric of daily life.

City directories listing the addresses of the inhabitants date from the 18th century, but the first *telephone* directory was issued in New Haven, Connecticut, in 1878. It consisted of a single sheet of cardboard printed with the names of the 50 individuals and businesses that had telephones in the local area.

The idea caught on quickly but it was another year before it occurred to anyone to arrange the list alphabetically or attach numbers to the individual telephones. That was recommended by a doctor from Lowell, Massachusetts, and only because he was paranoid that measles might wipe out the telephone exchange and the relief staff would need to be able to pick up their work with little training.

Telephone directories became a trusted institution; users relied on being able to scan them quickly to find the information they needed. This kind of utilitarian typesetting isn't often celebrated, but it is (or was) crucial, and in our opinion it should be.

Although it was a very modern-looking sans serif, the march of progress had doomed the original 1938 typeface Bell Gothic, designed by Chauncey H. Griffith. There were no issues when directories were printed on a letterpress using text composed by hot metal Linotype machinery, but it reproduced poorly under photographic cathode ray typesetting (CRT) technology combined with the high-speed offset lithography presses used in 1975.

One of the biggest problems was that lines thinned or disappeared altogether at the intersections of straight and curved strokes. When printers tried to compensate by over-inking the printing plates, letterforms bled into each other. Lowercase 'c' and 'l' read as 'd'; 'r' and 'n' became 'm'; '3' and '5' were often indistinguishable from '8' and '6'. The consequences for directory users were potentially dire. Excess ink also meant that presses had to be stopped and cleaned more frequently, costing time and money.

Readers of a certain age will remember telephone books – very handy for killing spiders.

Aa Bb Cc Dd Ee
Ff Gg Hh Ii Jj Kk

Bell Gothic

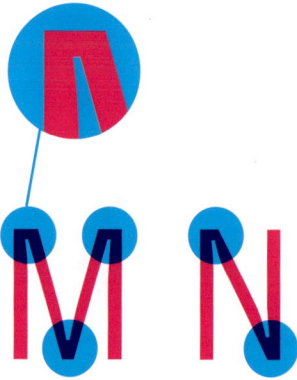

Ink traps in Bell Centennial

Carter's brief can be reasonably described as challenging: the new typeface needed to fit more characters per line without any loss of legibility, reduce the need for abbreviations and two-line entries, as well as reduce paper usage and overcome poor reproduction due to high-speed printing on newsprint. Phew.

It's a trap!

Carter's solution was manifold, and demonstrated his profound understanding of both type forms and the technicalities of printing. Carter designed four styles: Name and Number, Address, Sub Caption and Bold Listing. Linotype technology requires a letter to be the same width at different weights, whereas CRT reproduction allows greater variation. So Carter made the Name and Number face heavier and wider, and the Address face narrower and lighter, which established a more defined visual hierarchy within a tighter space.

He designed every character at the exact size (six point) it would be reproduced, using quadrille graph paper to represent each pixel. The presence or absence of a single tile on the grid would affect the shape of a curve or the angle of a stroke.

Carter increased the x-height and slightly condensed the character widths, while at the same time opening up the counterforms and bowls. He also squared off the slanted stroke ends of Bell Gothic to make Bell Centennial better complement Helvetica, used for the AT&T's corporate identity. The fun job of applying Bézier curves to the grid tiles for each character was given to the designer Alex Kaczun.

Carter's most important, and elegant, innovation was the incorporation of ink traps within most characters. These are where corners or small details are removed from within the letterforms in such a way that they will fill in with ink when printed. Any irregularities in the strokes of characters are invisible at small sizes. Bell Gothic included limited ink traps, for example in the uppercase 'M' and 'N', but for his typeface Carter treated them in a more methodical and refined way.

(opposite) These images compare the original drawings (top) to the digitized version (bottom). These pages are from a rare booklet lent by Carter to the Center for Design and Typography at the Cooper Union, New York.

The encoded numbers were proofed on a Versatec hard-copy printer. These Versatec bit-maps were checked against Carter's original drawings to confirm that shape, alignment and fit were correct. At this stage Carter made revisions at a video terminal.

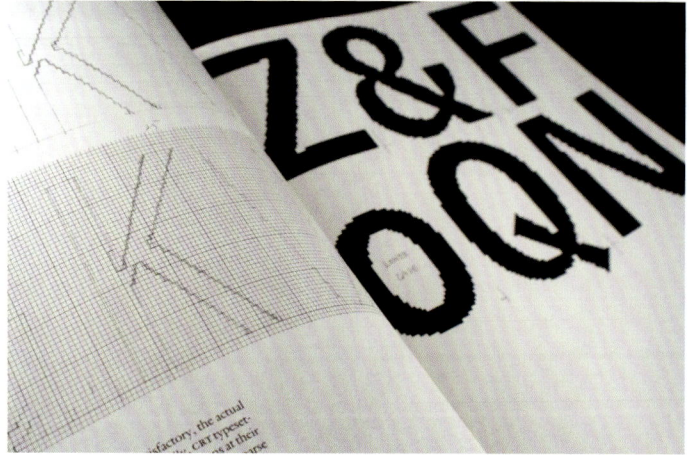

A close-up of the 'on or off' pixel-level decisions Carter made for Bell Centennial.

Bell curves

Bell Centennial is classified as a 'Lineal Grotesque' under the Vox type classification system. The stroke modulation is most evident in the lowercase characters. In keeping with others in this category, the uppercase 'G' features a spur, and the lowercase set combines a two-storey 'a' with a single-storey 'g'.

Carter transferred some elements across from Bell Gothic, namely the horizontal stroke across the top of the numeral '1', and the square tittles on the lowercase 'i' and 'j'. However, he made other changes to evoke the look of Helvetica by narrowing the lowercase 't' and 'f'.

b h k   G   a g

stroke modulation   *spur on 'G'*   *two-storey 'a'   single-storey 'g'*

l i j   l i j   t f   t f   t f

Bell Gothic   *Bell Centennial*   *Bell Gothic*   *Bell Centennial*   *Helvetica*

Bell Centennial in the wild

This typeface was created for a very specific purpose, so there are very few examples of its use outside of the AT&T telephone directory. However, because it sets so well at very small sizes, it's a good choice if you are in a jam and need to squish a lot of information into a small space.

There is no doubt that Matthew Carter nailed a very complex and exacting brief. The particular technological and reproduction problems that the ink trap design addresses need not be a consideration for other uses, and in no way interfere with the functionality of the typeface.

Only someone with the skills of Matthew Carter could turn a mechanical obstacle into something approaching a work of art.

Kiss, date, marry or kill?

Just like Tywin Lannister after his fatal bathroom break, telephone books have come to an untimely end. But just because we don't have telephone books any more shouldn't mean we can't have Bell Centennial in our lives. It is a perfectly valid and legible choice for body text, especially if size and spacing is a concern.

Although it's true that Bell Centennial does have quite a specific look at larger sizes, because the ink traps are evident, this aspect does not lack appeal. Designers have been known to blow Bell Centennial up to large sizes just to show off the ink traps (and because designers are just like that). Used in this way there is something fluid and vibrant about the letterforms, reminiscent of Henri Matisse's figurative posters, such as *Icarus* or *La Danse*; something organic and fleeting, just like a kiss.

And this is exactly what we choose to do with Bell Centennial.

Foundry Sterling

Designers: Freda Sack and David Quay
Date: 2002

Portrait of Freda Sack.

Before computer-generated design, students often had what could be described as a love-hate relationship with Letraset, a dry transfer lettering method. On the one hand, it gave our projects a professional look and there was something satisfyingly therapeutic about rubbing the film to transfer the lettering; on the other hand, there was the frustration of peeling back a letter that hadn't attached properly, leaving bits like stray filaments to ruin the finish, or discovering you had run out of copies of that one crucial character.

This produced a quiet generational trauma — Letraset sheets were not cheap.

In this chapter we will highlight the typeface Foundry Sterling, and in so doing profile the uncrowned queen of Letraset, the late, great Freda Sack.

Buckley, and then some

Born Freda Buckley in Enfield, north London, in 1951, Sack attended the Kent School of Printing at Maidstone College of Art, where she trained in traditional typography, typesetting and print technology. Here she developed hand type-drawing skills. At the age of 21 Sack successfully interviewed at the nearby Letraset Studio in Ashford for a trainee position. The Letraset type studio was unionized, and in order to obtain her union card she spent six months in the photography studio, retouching and readying lettering sheets for the dry transfer process.

After becoming a stencil-cutter and then type designer at Letraset, Sack worked for two years at FONTS/Hardy Williams Design in London in the late 1970s. In 1980 she returned briefly to Letraset to expand the range of new digital typefaces and improve their version of the typography software Ikarus to make it more intuitive and user-friendly.

abcdefghijklm
nopqrstuvwxyz
ABCDEFGHIJKLM
NOPQRSTUVWXYZ
0123456789!?

abcdefghijklm
nopqrstuvwxyz
ABCDEFGHIJKLM
NOPQRSTUVWXYZ
0123456789!?

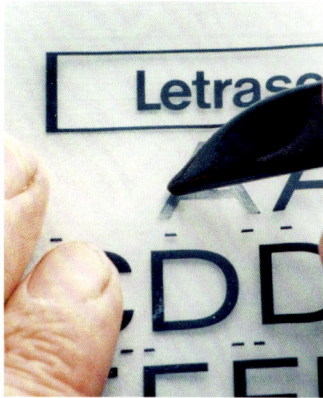

The advertised experience of Letraset.

Sack struck out on her own in 1983 with a stable of freelance clients that included British Airways, NatWest Bank, Vauxhall Motors and *The Daily Telegraph*. During this time she designed Brunel, a typeface used by every mainline railway station in the UK.

In 1989 she teamed up with David Quay and Mike Daines from the technical and distribution company Signus to set up The Foundry, the first independent type foundry in the UK. In 1998 they took on fresh young graduate Stuart de Rozario to aid in the design and font production under their art direction, and he stayed on for 14 years. In 2012 Freda continued with her own independent company Foundry Types, which focused on expanding The Foundry typeface library. Distribution was handled by Monotype, allowing her to focus on the design work until she shut up shop in 2014.

Sack lectured at the Glasgow School of Art, Cumbria College of Art and Design, Nottingham Trent University and Bournemouth and Poole College of Art and Design, and sat on the Board of Governors of the University of Creative Arts. She was a longtime member of the International Society of Typographic Designers, and was appointed co-chair with Quay from 1995 to 1999, chair from 2000 to 2004, and president from 2006 to 2010.

Sack was made an honorary fellow of the society in 2018, shortly before her death the following year. Her many obituaries are testament to the impact she had on the design community, all of them mentioning her warmth, generosity and support for young designers.

Life at Letraset

Letraset was founded in the UK in 1959 and initially sold wet transfer lettering similar to scale-model decals before introducing their dry transfer lettering products in 1961. The company is now a subsidiary of the art supplies manufacturer Winsor & Newton.

In several key ways Letraset's impact on graphic design in the 1960s and 70s was as revolutionary as digital technology in later decades. Hand lettering was painstaking and time-consuming, and screen printing was expensive and often impractical, particularly for mock-ups. Suddenly, Letraset provided designers with access to entire alphabets of uniformly sized and shaped letters. And if mistakes were made, with care (and practice) the letters could be removed or even repositioned — you only had to undo rather than start over.

Of course, the process wasn't infallible. Care and patience could only take you so far, because Letraset rather famously also sucked. Apply too little pressure and the letters would not stick firmly, leaving only half a character on the page. Apply too much pressure and the other letters you already transferred would reattach themselves to the sheet. This nightmare was compounded when you realized that the letters you need to fix the problem had been ruined. Many left-handers are still in therapy because of their Letraset experience.

Letraset had a reputation for being a bit naff, but it's worth remembering that it was taken up in a big way by the punk movement. Its appeal lay in both the DIY approach and the quality of the end result, producing designs independent of the mainstream. So, street cred where credit is due.

Trainees at the Letraset company undertook what was effectively a five-year 'apprenticeship'. In his 2018 book, *Letraset*, the writer and graphic designer Adrian Shaughnessy interviewed Sack, who described making her own basic tools — which sounds like an inmate from a prison drama crafting a shiv:

> *The first thing we had to do was make our own knife — essentially a long piece of wood with a piece of metal type as a counter balance at one end, and a single-edged razor blade taped to the side at an angle to enable the edge, up to a certain level, and the point, to be manipulated freehand; depending on whether you held the knife near to the blade end or at the far end of the 'handle' this would give access to a range of curves from very tight to long shallow sweeps — the knife being held relatively still while the Rubylith itself was pivoted around by your other hand. Sounds crazy — but it worked.*

Improvised tools for making stencils.

Letraset designers used sorts as references to create the artwork for existing typefaces and were expected to draw any missing characters to match; a process that relied on meticulous detail and an accurate eye.

It took one person four to six weeks to draw, cut and space one typeface, consisting of a headline character set in one weight or style. This involved measuring and analysing all the aspects and features, before creating a template and drawing the outlines of the individual glyphs. The designers worked at 100–150mm cap height, or larger for more intricate designs. The Rubylith was then cut, and the characters individually spaced by eye and hand on vertical lightboxes.

New and original concepts for typefaces could be submitted by both in-house and external designers, type enthusiasts or competition winners. Sometimes there were only basic marker sketches or rough small-scale drawings for the Letraset team to work from. This experience enabled Sack to identify any typeface placed in front of her, and develop her famously innate understanding of proportions and structure.

Sterling by name, sterling by nature

Foundry Sterling was designed in 2001 and released in 2002. The original concept for the typeface developed from Sack's Brunel typeface — commissioned by the British railway company Railtrack — and another designed for British Gas, but with a greater focus on more humanist proportions and the purity of the lines.

In interviews after Sack's death, both Quay and de Rozario suggest she was reluctant to make Foundry Sterling but came around after some persuasion. Quay described the design process at The Foundry as 85% of the ideas coming from his sketches and initial concepts (and presumably skilled arguments to convince Sack).

Now, we don't have a direct account from Sack to describe in detail how Foundry Sterling was created, but we do have her description of how things worked at The Foundry, and it is slightly different. Sack describes Quay as a skilled hand letterer and indicates that making a logo or a word in custom hand lettering is a different skill to creating an entire letter set that worked together; Sack provided the ability to turn his ideas into full typefaces. She described the process of forming a partnership with Quay as coming about because they had so many telephone calls about the minutiae of letter proportions that it was easier to set up in a studio so they could sketch side by side, sharing their work until it was perfect.

If the basis of Foundry Sterling was Sack's earlier work, reconstructed by Quay's sketches and reconstituted by de Rozario on the computer, then who should be credited as the principal designer? A fascinating question for the ages, and yet another example of how typeface authorship can be complicated.

The typeface was released in seven weights from light to extra bold. It is a sans serif, and within the Vox classification system is categorized as a 'Lineal Neo-grotesque'. Typical of this class, it has little stroke contrast and the terminals on the curves, such as the 'C' and the lowercase 'g', are slanted. The uppercase 'G' has no spur.

Foundry Sterling has enough substance and distinction to work as a headline, while producing a balanced grey when set as body copy. Even in the heavier weights it avoids the chunkiness and clunkiness of other typefaces, which is a testament to Sack's mastery of the letterform.

angled terminals on the curves   *spurless 'G'*

Foundry Sterling in the wild

The most high-profile use of this typeface in corporate branding is for the University of Oxford. If you're looking for a crisp and quality addition that won't clash with centuries of tradition like some tacky parvenu, you can't go past Foundry Sterling.

The typeface also appeared on wayfinding signage at Berlin Schönefeld Airport, which probably made a pleasant change from the more industrial and Teutonic members of the DIN family.

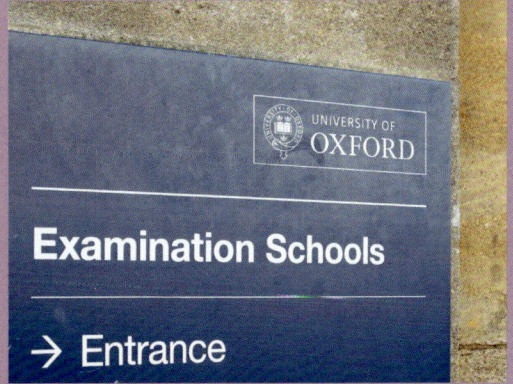

(above) Oxford University signage, where Foundry Sterling features in the university branding.
(below) Wayfinding signage at Berlin Airport.

Transport

Designers: Margaret Calvert and Jock Kinneir
Date: 1958

Portrait of Margaret Calvert.

The freeway approach to most modern cities is formulaic. Even if you've never visited before, there is a familiarity to the combination of concrete, steel and bitumen channelling the flow of traffic. Regularly placed wayfinding signs, usually sans serif against a colour-coded background, give drivers some confidence in navigating the individual urban geography. That sense of confidence owes a great deal to the work of Margaret Calvert and her mentor and longtime collaborator, Richard 'Jock' Kinneir.

Not only did Calvert make her mark in the world of type design, but she was also equally influential in the design of pictograms. Which is how she made her signature bob one of the most recognizable hairstyles on the planet (take that, Rachel Green from *Friends*!)

Don't ask Margaret Calvert to type

Born in South Africa in 1936, Margaret Calvert moved with her family to London in 1950. She enrolled at the Chelsea College of Art where, after a two-year intermediate course in sculpture, painting and life drawing, she chose printmaking and illustration. This introduced her to Jock Kinneir, one of several guest graphic designers invited by the college to set projects for students.

Nineteen-year-old Calvert's enthusiasm for lettering and illustration drew Kinneir's attention as he was looking for someone to assist in his practice with the design for signage at London's Gatwick Airport. As sometimes happens, that job offer fell through almost immediately, but after a chance meeting between Calvert and Kinneir at Ealing Broadway railway station, the invitation was renewed. When she asked him what the work would involve, he stated, 'Absolutely nothing like what you've been doing at Chelsea.' Who doesn't like hearing that work will be nothing like school? The company eventually expanded and was renamed Kinneir Calvert Tuhill.

abcdefghijklm
nopqrstuvwxyz
ABCDEFGHIJKLM
NOPQRSTUVWXYZ
0123456789 $\frac{1}{2}$ $\frac{3}{4}$ & ?

abcdefghijklm
nopqrstuvwxyz
ABCDEFGHIJKLM
NOPQRSTUVWXYZ
0123456789 ! ?

New Transport Light for light on dark backgrounds   Margaret Calvert April 2012

(above) Original drawings of Transport.

(right) A young Margaret Calvert and Jock Kinneir play with some P&O playing cards designed by Margaret (note the bob).

(opposite) In an episode of the BBC's car show *Top Gear*, Calvert and May found an unattended 'Man at Work' (aka 'Man Opening Umbrella'), which May defaced to make the shovel more shovel-like as Calvert looked on. For the record, to this day Calvert remains happy with her original design.

Calvert worked at a time when design was dominated by men, and — as she put it — women were hired mainly for how good they looked in a miniskirt. Calvert chose another path, deliberately being bad at 'women's work' such as typing so she wouldn't be asked to do it, and always insisting on the validity of her opinions. By her own account, Kinneir always respected those opinions.

As well as her work at Kinneir Calvert Tuhill, Calvert designed typefaces for Monotype and taught at the Royal College of Art for nearly 40 years, where she headed the graphics department from 1987 to 1991. She has received honorary degrees and fellowships as well as awards for design excellence, including her appointment in 2016 as an Officer of the Order of the British Empire (OBE) for services to typography and road safety. The Design Museum London hosted a retrospective of her work from 2020 to 2021. In 2020 Calvert released Rail Alphabet 2, designed with another frequent collaborator, Henrik Kubel, which is a new version of the typeface used for the UK rail system.

The signs are all around us

Calvert's most famous works are pictograms for the road warning signs introduced by the British Ministry of Transport in 1965. She drew (literally) on her own experience for this work: the deer crossing was inspired by Eadweard Muybridge's footage of animals in motion, which she'd seen in college; the cow pictogram warning of farm animals was based on a cousin's cow named Patience; both of the children in the 'Children Crossing' sign are representations of Calvert, immortalizing herself (and her bob haircut).

These road signs have made their way deep into the public consciousness. Calvert appeared on Season 14 of the British TV series *Top Gear*, where she was driven around and interviewed by host James May.

THE HIGHWAY CODE

ESSENTIAL FOR ALL DRIVERS

FULLY UPDATED & COMPLETE

PLUS TAKING YOUR DRIVING TEST — WHAT TO EXPECT

UP-TO-DATE RULES OF THE ROAD FOR ALL DRIVERS

KEY INFORMATION FOR ALL ROAD USERS INCLUDING CYCLISTS AND MOTORCYCLISTS

Don't mention the war

Calvert is adamant that the original Transport was never a typeface. Nevertheless, it was part of an overhaul of existing signage, a job so important it affected everybody. Prior to 1957, British road signage consisted of 'fingerpost' signs utilizing a variety of sans serif typefaces, and banner signs printed in all caps in Llewellyn-Smith — also known as 'Ministry' (short for the Ministry of Transport).

In 1957 the Ministry of Transport established the Advisory Committee on Traffic Signs. Kinneir was appointed to oversee the design direction, with Calvert ably assisting — such as when she presented to the Worboys Committee (reviewing the traffic signs for all-purpose roads), while Kinneir was sick with the flu. The original commission suggested a look similar to contemporary German typefaces like DIN 1451, in use for the German motorway system since before World War II. Kinneir and Calvert rejected this direction as being unsympathetic to the British countryside (we're not saying memories lingered on from the war, but you can draw your own conclusions).

They created two original lettering styles: Transport Medium, for white text on dark backgrounds, and Transport Heavy, for black text on white backgrounds. Technically these were not yet full typefaces, but they did include certain symbols: apostrophes, the pound sign, vulgar fractions without the horizontal bar to improve legibility, and some diacritics for the Welsh and Irish languages. The signage was initially tested on the Preston bypass (now part of the M6) in 1958, and introduced on the London—Yorkshire motorway (M1) in 1959.

Trial by media

Importantly, the designs for the new motorway signs were published in *The Times* in 1958. A Cambridge-based letter-cutter and sculptor named David Kindersley led a backlash. We refer to a couple of 'typography wars' in this book, and if this wasn't a pitched battle, then it was definitely a serious skirmish.

Kindersley was a rival of team Kinneir/Calvert. He worked for the Ministry of Transport in the early 1950s and designed Kindersley MOT, a serif typeface based on Trajan for use on street name signs. In a very British way, this dispute played out over the next few years in the press; the phrase 'the thin end of the wedge' was doubtless thrown down several times in letters to editors.

Kindersley and his supporters insisted his all-caps typeface was not only more legible and elegant, but it also made more efficient use of space and the signage could therefore be smaller and more economical. Kinneir and Calvert believed that drivers travelling at speed would not spell out individual letters and hence needed a pattern

(above) Ministry was a condensed typeface inspired by Gill Sans and used by the railways.

(opposite) Calvert's signage is very familiar to drivers.

Maquettes for the Transport road
signage showing the white and dark
versions of the lettering.

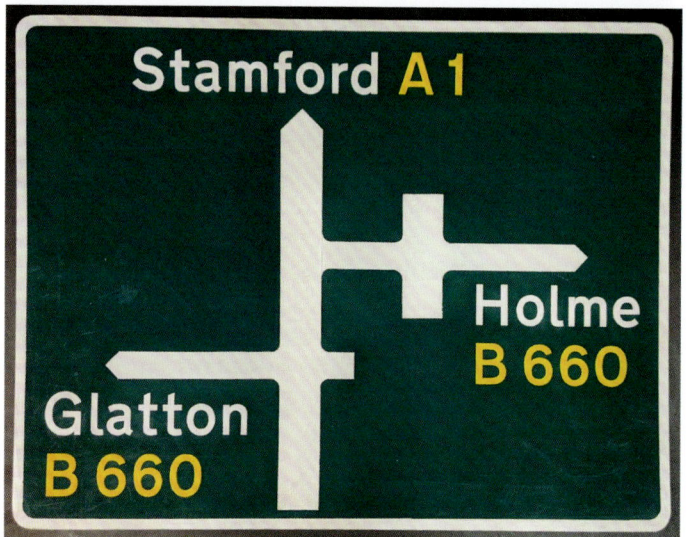

of ascenders and descenders in order to recognize the *shape* of a word. According to their theory, all-caps signage would create a useless and indistinguishable rectangle of letters.

A jury of airmen

Eventually, in an effort to resolve the dispute, the Roads Research Laboratory set up a series of legibility trials at Benson Airport in 1961. These consisted of mocked-up road signs in four styles — Transport at two sizes and Kindersley MOT with and without serifs — driven at speed towards a grandstand of seated airmen.

To the surprise of no one with a firm grasp of scientific rigour, the results were inconclusive. At this point in her recollections, Calvert *really* sticks the boot in, dissing the Kindersley MOT typeface as being 'just so ugly'. The committee eventually chose the more modern Transport. Aesthetics won the day, a shocking victory from the modern perspective of the bottom-line outweighing most other considerations.

Lest you think David Kindersley has been unfairly consigned to the dustbin of history, his work has been immortalized on film — for example, in the opening scene of the first Harry Potter film, the street sign (and sometime owl perch) for Privet Drive uses Kindersley MOT.

The one photo that exists of the Benson Airport research doesn't inspire confidence, given that no one is actually attempting to read the test sign.

It's Akzidenz-Grotesk until it isn't

Calvert admits that Transport was originally based on Akzidenz-Grotesk, with her and Kinneir making whatever alterations they felt were required to the letterforms, particularly the terminals, to improve their suitability for this new and specific purpose.

Some of the key changes that were made reduced the length of the ascenders and descenders in relation to the x-height and narrowed uppercase characters such as the 'P' and 'R'. In terms of Vox classification, Transport is a 'Lineal Grotesque'.

New Transport, the updated and extended version of the typeface released by Calvert and Henrik Kubel in 2021, features thin, light, regular, medium, bold and black faces, along with complementary obliques (italics).

cap height
x-height

baseline

ascenders and descenders of Transport vs Akzidenz-Grotesk

character width of Transport vs Akzidenz-Grotesk

Transport in the wild

Transport has expanded well beyond British highways and byways and is used for road signage around the world, from Iceland to India, Greece and large areas of the Middle East to Singapore. Two European countries use local, bolder variants, which are known as 'Alfabeto Normale' in Italy and 'Carretera Convencional' in Spain.

It would be easy to peg Transport as a one-use wonder, no matter how ubiquitous that usage might be. We might quibble over the science of Kinneir and Calvert's methods, but the fact remains that their lettering system was tested, and in ways that might have defeated a less considered design. They pioneered not only a new look for signage with Transport, but also the comprehensive overhaul of an entire information communication system. In many ways and places it has been a highly successful British export, and where it hasn't been used itself, it has influenced the look and design of its equivalents.

Given its very specific use, should you change your default settings to Transport?

Kiss, date, marry or kill?

Away from its wayfinding context, Transport remains a clean, modern, versatile and attractive sans serif design. It pairs very well with other typefaces and stands up equally well on its own merits.

If it were an actor, Transport would be famous for its classically trained Shakespearean repertoire while easily making the transition to lighter film roles. Think of someone like Dame Judi Dench. And who wouldn't treasure a kiss from the legendary but down-to-earth Dame Judi?

Or perhaps we should give the last word to Margaret Calvert herself, who has hinted that while she and Jock never set out to rebrand the UK, their contribution has become as quintessential as London black cabs or red buses.

(right) Datto Inc., the US cybersecurity and data company, uses New Transport Medium for its logotype.

(opposite) Transport on road signage in Iceland (top) and India (bottom).

| 225 | Akureyri | 1 | | 1 | Reykjavík | 163 |
| 34 | Hvammstangi | 72 | | 1 | Borgarnes | 90 |

पाली Pali	58
सोजत Sojat	18
पिण्डवाड़ा Pindwara	192

✳❀◻❆ ♣❉■✳❂❀ ▼▲ (Zapf Dingbats)

Designer: Hermann Zapf
Date: 1978

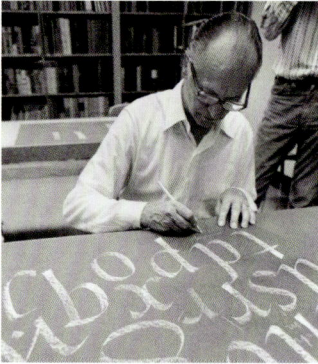

Hermann Zapf at work.

If a group of symbols can be set like letters, can we call it a typeface? If that same set of symbols communicates meaning — in some ways better than letters do — hasn't it earned the right to be called a typeface? These are questions for the ages, which this chapter does not even attempt to answer. Instead, we would like to talk about Zapf Dingbats. Because Zapf Dingbats is part of the reason that we use the @ symbol to write email addresses, and when it became part of Unicode it paved the way for the emoji.

Zapf Dingbats is kind of a big deal, but we used and loved it since before it became internet famous.

A birth surrounded by death

Zapf Dingbats is the work of the remarkable Hermann Zapf, a man described as having unsurpassed muscle fluidity. Calligrapher, typeface designer, teacher and digital type pioneer, Zapf had a long career spanning (and contributing to) the major technological advancements of typography in the 20th century.

Zapf described the circumstances of his birth as 'chaotic', which sounds dramatic, but in fact we think he may have been understating it. Born in Germany in 1918, he narrowly missed World War I, arriving just in time for the post-war 'November Revolution' of 1919. The Spanish flu epidemic was raging, killing two of his brothers, and in 1925 his hometown of Nuremberg suffered a famine. Nuremberg would later become the site of the famous Nazi trials following World War II, and Hermann lived through the rise and fall of the Nazis, too.

In short, Zapf's early life was lived around a lot of death, so it's perhaps not surprising that Optima, one of his most famous typefaces, is often used for memorials and gravestones. This typographic achievement was years in his future, however: first he had to get through school.

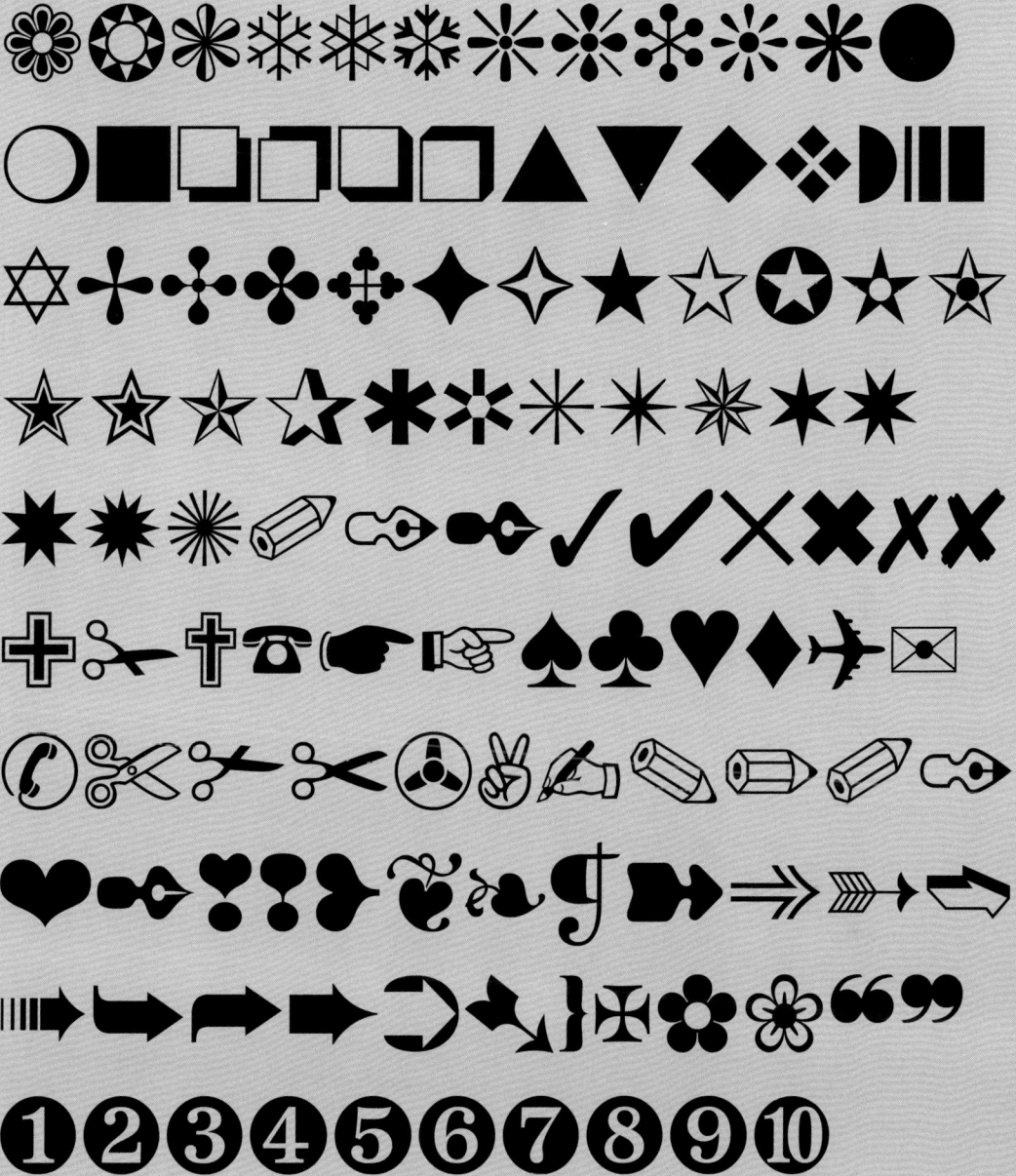

Zapf Dingbats featured in Lubalin's
U&lc magazine (1978), where you get a
good sense of how the forms captured
the zeitgeist.

Zapf was considered the son of a 'subversive', which limited his education options. His father, a trade unionist, was arrested, lost his job and spent time in the Dachau concentration camp. The young Zapf wanted to be an electrical engineer, but because of his father was unable to attend the Ohm-Polytechnical Institute. From an early age he was a skilled draughtsman, so his teachers suggested he try for an apprenticeship in lithography instead. Dare we say it, we think he would have been wasted as an electrical engineer (don't @ us, electrical engineers!)

In Nazi Germany in 1933, you would be asked political questions at each job interview. Hermann was rejected by everyone and only managed to secure an apprenticeship at the very last company in the telephone directory. The company, which either had decent politics or an ineffective HR department, didn't ask any awkward questions and gave Zapf a job as an apprentice photo retoucher. Inspired by an exhibition of work by the famous typographer Rudolf Koch in 1935, Zapf bought two of his books and taught himself calligraphy. His bosses noticed and put him in charge of lettering, and he was on his way to a career in typography.

Zapf moved to Frankfurt at the end of his apprenticeship and secured a role at the Werkstatt Haus zum Fürsteneck, run by Koch's son, Paul Koch. Here he created typography for sheet music and got to know people at the two major type foundries: D. Stempel AG and Linotype GmbH. Zapf designed his first typeface, the blackletter Gilgengart, for Stempel in 1938. The use of this typeface was banned, along with all other blackletter typefaces, by the Nazis in 1941.

Zapf was conscripted into the army during World War II, landing in the artillery where his hand skills did not translate into gun skills. After confusing left with right and being too slow and clumsy, he was sent off to the cartography division and spent the rest of the war making maps. He was great at this, able to draw 1mm-high hand lettering without a magnifying glass. Well played, Hermann — because anyone who can do that can probably fire a gun pretty accurately, too.

After the war Zapf started teaching calligraphy and settled in Frankfurt, where he was appointed head of the print shop at Stempel. It's here, in 1948, that he met his wife and fellow calligraphy teacher Gudrun von Hesse. She was an accomplished professional calligrapher, bookbinder, punchcutter and type designer. In a refreshing change for this book, she did not combine her career with her husband's; instead, she ran her own bookbindery in the grounds of Stempel. In 2018, at the age of 100, she released her first digital typeface — a cut of her typeface Hesse Antiqua, originally designed for gilt stamped bookbinding.

(right) Zapf sketched his idea for Optima onto an Italian lira.

(below) Memorial plaques on the floor of the Santa Croce church, Florence, showing inscriptions that inspired Zapf to create Optima.

(opposite) Optima's most famous application is on the Vietnam Veterans Memorial in Washington DC, and later (maybe not coincidentally) for the US senator and Vietnam veteran John McCain's 2008 presidential bid.

Gudrun was presumably present on the 1951 holiday to Florence when Hermann found inspiration on a gravestone to design Optima. Optima was released in 1958, and it's fair to say that it divides opinions. Many designers love Optima for its classic lines and lovely letters 'Q' and 'Y'; others dislike it because it can't decide whether it's a serif or sans serif.

The list of Hermann Zapf's typefaces is long and includes Aldus, Zapf Chancery and the extravagant script face Zapfino. Perhaps his best-known typeface is Palatino, designed in 1948. In his later years Zapf focused on making digital versions of his earlier work, redesigning them to get rid of the compromises made for metal type.

Throughout his life Zapf practised calligraphy as both a teacher and artist (rather than professionally, like Gudrun). He served as a consultant to Hallmark cards, and you can see his amazing hand skills in action in a film they made: *The Art of Hermann Zapf.*

Zapf wrote numerous books, including *Alphabet Stories*, *About Alphabets* and *Manuale Typographicum*. Zapf won the Frederic W. Goudy award in 1969 and the Gutenberg Prize in 1974. He worked well into his 90s, and died in Darmstadt, Germany, in 2015. Zapf's niece made a film about Hermann and Gudrun called *Alphabet Magic* in 2019.

Chancery

Zapfino

Palatino

Haste not, want not

Hermann Zapf started working in computer typography in the 1960s, the fulfilment of his dream to be an engineer. His contribution to computer typography is too long to do justice to in this book. This work took him to the USA where, in 1976, Zapf became a professor of typographic computer programming for the Rochester Institute of Technology. The following year he formed Design Processing International (DPI) with New York type designers Herb Lubalin and Aaron Burns to develop typographic computer software.

In 1977 Zapf, Lubalin and Burns had a conversation about developing a group of symbols and signs into a typeface for ITC. Zapf was able to draw on a personal collection of more than 1,200 designs he had sketched over many years. From these, 360 symbols and ornamental characters were selected and divided into three sets, each containing 120 glyphs, and named the ITC-100, ITC-200 and ITC-300 series. ITC rushed the release of the Zapf Dingbats series in the spring of 1978, giving Zapf very little time to make improvements or corrections to the designs — a disappointment that haunted him despite its commercial success. In his words, you can't make a good typeface under the pressure of time.

Zapf Dingbats influenced the development of other dingbat typefaces, most notably Wingdings (the name is a portmanteau of 'Windows' and 'dingbats'); this was designed by Charles Bigelow and Kris Holmes, themselves protégés of Zapf, and released by Microsoft in 1992.

Steve Jobs was a Zapf fan, and gave Hermann his first Apple Mac in 1984. Zapf Dingbats was then included in the 35 typefaces written into Postscript, kicking off 'desktop publishing' when the Apple LaserWriter printer was released in 1986. Zapf Dingbats later contributed symbols to Unicode's typographical ornaments block, part of Unicode's goal to create a universal character set across languages and symbols. Today, Unicode encodes most web pages and supports emojis, solving compatibility issues across digital locales and platforms.

It isn't a stretch to see a logical progression from the introduction of digital dingbats to emoticons and thence to emojis (just for the record, any association with the English 'emotion' is purely coincidental, as the Japanese word is formed from '*e*', meaning picture, and '*moji*', character). And the trend for replacing words and concepts with pictograms and images brings us full circle back to the very origins of writing itself. So in a way, although Zapf Dingbats marks the advent of modern digital technology, it takes us back to our roots more than any other typeface in this book.

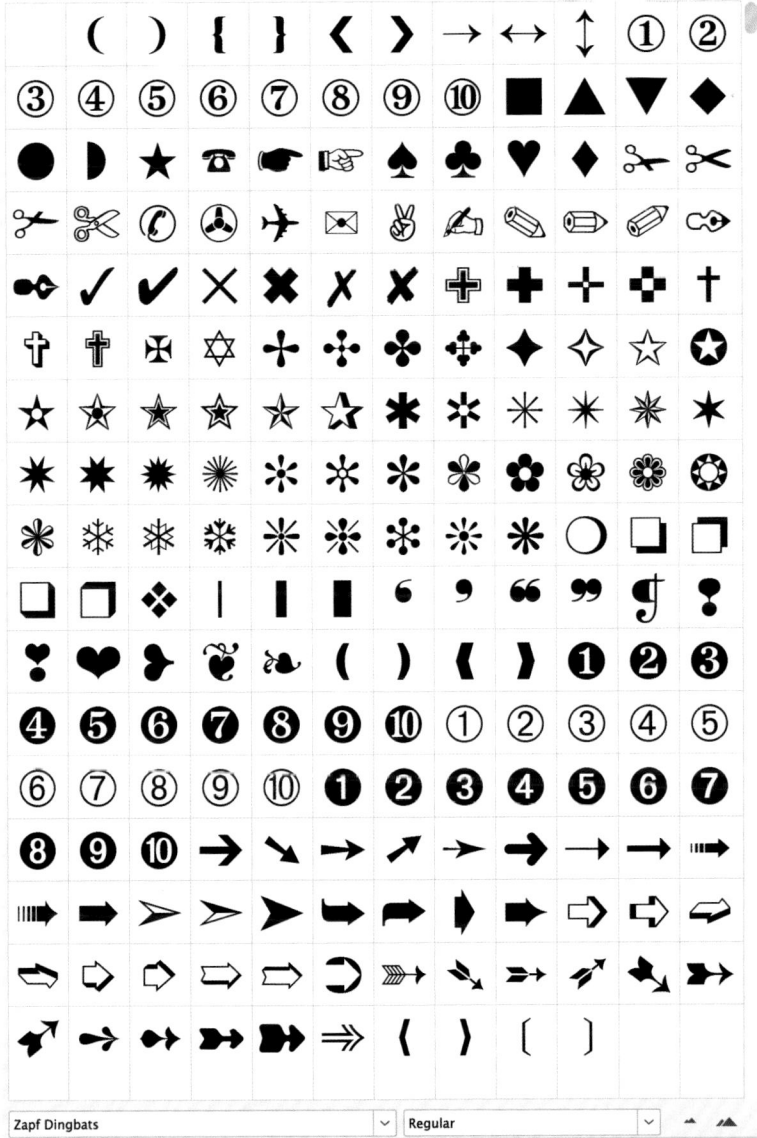

Zapf Dingbats | Regular

What's in a name?

The word 'dingbat' has a motley etymology. It has come to mean, variously, a strong alcoholic drink, a coin or banknote, an idiot or eccentric person, a name for various unspecified objects or gadgets (think 'thingummy') and the male genitalia. Its origins are supposedly Danish, Dutch or German. The notion that it represents the sound of a metal sort striking the print room floor seems implausibly corny to us.

For typographic purposes, a dingbat is generally defined as a glyph other than a letter or a number (confusingly, some dingbats are different shapes containing numbers), used for the replacement of text or for ornamentation. They often take the form of natural motifs, stars, arrows, solid and outlined geometric shapes, and segments that can be aligned to form box frames or a horizontal break between paragraphs.

Dingbats don't have anatomy in the traditional sense. The flowers and leaf types, called florets or fleurons, are derived from manuscript decorations drawn by medieval scribes. The various hand gestures, or 'manicules', hark back to even earlier, classical Roman origins. Depending on the set, other glyphs might include more modern implements like scissors, pens and nibs, and envelopes, through to inventions like the telephone and aeroplane.

No anatomy to show, so let's take the opportunity to admire a few of the best dingbats in Zapf Dingbats.

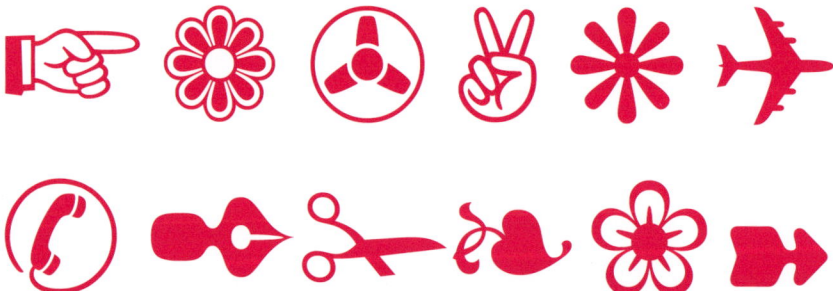

Zapf Dingbats in the wild

Zapf Dingbats was considered so significant it became one of the 14 basic typefaces incorporated into all PDF files. The scissor icon is often used on paper forms to indicate where to cut.

You can of course find dingbats in Unicode by popping up the glyph palette. One of the most famous uses of Zapf Dingbats as a typeface was when David Carson used it in 1994 to set a 'boring' Bryan Ferry interview in *Raygun* magazine — arguably making it more interesting.

An old designer trick for creating (free!) design elements is to enlarge Zapf Dingbats, as seen here, where symbols replace letters in the masthead of *Spain Fashion* magazine.

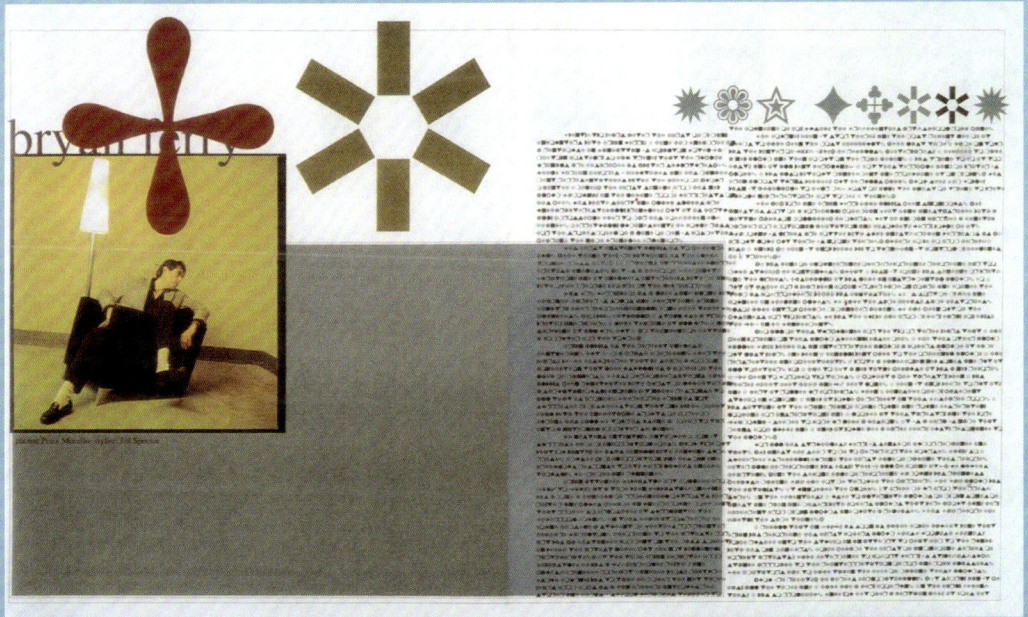

Kiss, date, marry or kill?

You can think of Zapf Dingbats as the typographic equivalent of garlic salt, providing a subtle flavour boost to your layouts (unless you are David Carson, obviously). Like that friend you invite around to add a little 'spice' to proceedings, it's guaranteed to kick off the party. Let's face it, if the old adage about a picture being worth a thousand words is true, then you don't get much more bang for your buck than with Zapf Dingbats.

Zapf Dingbats will always have our hearts, and we are especially partial to scissors 2701. Thanks for the vibes over all these years, Zapf Dingbats :)

(above) Indecipherable article about Bryan Ferry in *Raygun* magazine.

(right) Zapf Dingbats writ large in the masthead of a Spanish fashion mag.

(far right) Scissor icon on a mailing form.

Univers

Designer: Adrian Frutiger
Date: 1957

Adrian Frutiger at work.

When designers are looking for a minimalist, neutral typeface they invariably reach for Helvetica. When you're a design student, the hype around Helvetica can be so overwhelming it is almost impossible to question, and it's no surprise to us that Helvetica is the only typeface with its own movie. However, there are other typefaces that arguably do the job just as well — if not better — and Univers is one of those. Univers shares a birthday and a nationality (well, kind of) with Helvetica. At one point, Univers may have even come close to eclipsing Helvetica. This is the story of why it didn't.

Words and woodcuts

Adrian Frutiger, the designer of Univers, was born in Unterseen, in the canton of Bern, Switzerland, in 1928. The son of a weaver, he went to Gewerbeschule (a type of trade school) in Bern, where he studied woodcuts and drawing, and he had a keen interest in calligraphy, having invented several scripts as a child. Encouraged by his father not to become a fine artist, he leaned into his typographic side and was apprenticed to the Otto Schlaefli printshop in Interlaken at the age of 16.

Upon completing his apprenticeship, Frutiger was briefly employed as a metal type compositor at Gebrüder Fretz, a Zurich-based printing and publishing firm that produced posters, maps, periodicals and postcards. In 1949 he enrolled in the Kunstgewerbeschule (College of the Arts) in Zurich, in order to focus on typography. For his final year assignment he illustrated an essay entitled 'The Development of the Latin Alphabet' with woodcuts; on the basis of this he was recruited by a leading Parisian type foundry, Deberny & Peignot.

In the early 1960s Frutiger, still living in Paris, partnered up with Bruno Pfäffli and André Gürtler to establish their own graphic design studio. Their clientele included museums, art galleries and major French corporations.

abcdefghijklm
nopqrstuvwxyz
ABCDEFGHIJKLM
NOPQRSTUVWXYZ
0123456789!?

abcdefghijklm
nopqrstuvwxyz
ABCDEFGHIJKLM
NOPQRSTUVWXYZ
0123456789!?

Frutiger's notes giving measurements
for the typeface on a draft of Univers.

Univers

It looks like the studio was a fun place to work. This image from a 1967 New Year's greeting card from the studio features (l–r) Suzanne Curtil, Nicole Delamarre, Adrian Frutiger, Bruno Pfäffli and Sylvain Robin being jolly in Paris.

In 1963 Frutiger secured a major commission from the European Computer Manufacturers Association (ECMA). Based in Geneva, this organization wanted to develop a new standard for optical character recognition (OCR), the process by which printed text and numbers were captured and converted into electronic data. They wanted to improve on OCR-A, developed in the US, by generating a system that was both truly international and better able to integrate with future technologies. Frutiger's solution, OCR-B, was adopted in 1973. It is commonly found on UPC and ISBN barcodes, as well as most government-issued identity documents around the world, including passports.

(right and opposite) Frutiger's designs for the Paris Métro and Charles de Gaulle Airport in the 1970s using his typeface Univers.

In 1970 Frutiger began designing the signage system for the then new Charles de Gaulle Airport, which opened in 1974. Later he designed signage for the Paris Métro. He was responsible for more than 30 typefaces, embracing improved digital production methods in the 1990s to expand some of his most famous faces: Frutiger, Avenir and, of course, Univers.

Later commissions were diverse, ranging from a limited-edition watch face for the Hamilton Ventura to three stamps celebrating Swiss design for the Swiss Post Office.

Frutiger received several prestigious awards: both the Chevalier dans l'Ordre des Arts et des Lettres (1970) and the Officier de l'Ordre des Arts et des Lettres (1990), a gold medal from the Type Directors Club, New York (1987), and elevation to the European Design Hall of Fame (voted by a jury of journalists and critics from 15 design magazines) in 2009.

Frutiger's personal life was sadly tragic by anyone's standards. His first wife, Paulette, died after giving birth to their son only two years in to their marriage. His second marriage produced two daughters, both of whom suffered mental health issues and died by suicide as teenagers. He and his second wife, Simone, established a foundation in their honour, which still funds research and suicide-prevention efforts today. We hope that the foundation, his strong Calvinist faith (and, we like to think, his passion for typography) provided some solace to Frutiger.

Adrian Frutiger died in 2015 at the ripe old age of 87, after a storied career spanning the complete transition of typography from metal through photo composition to digital.

Univers

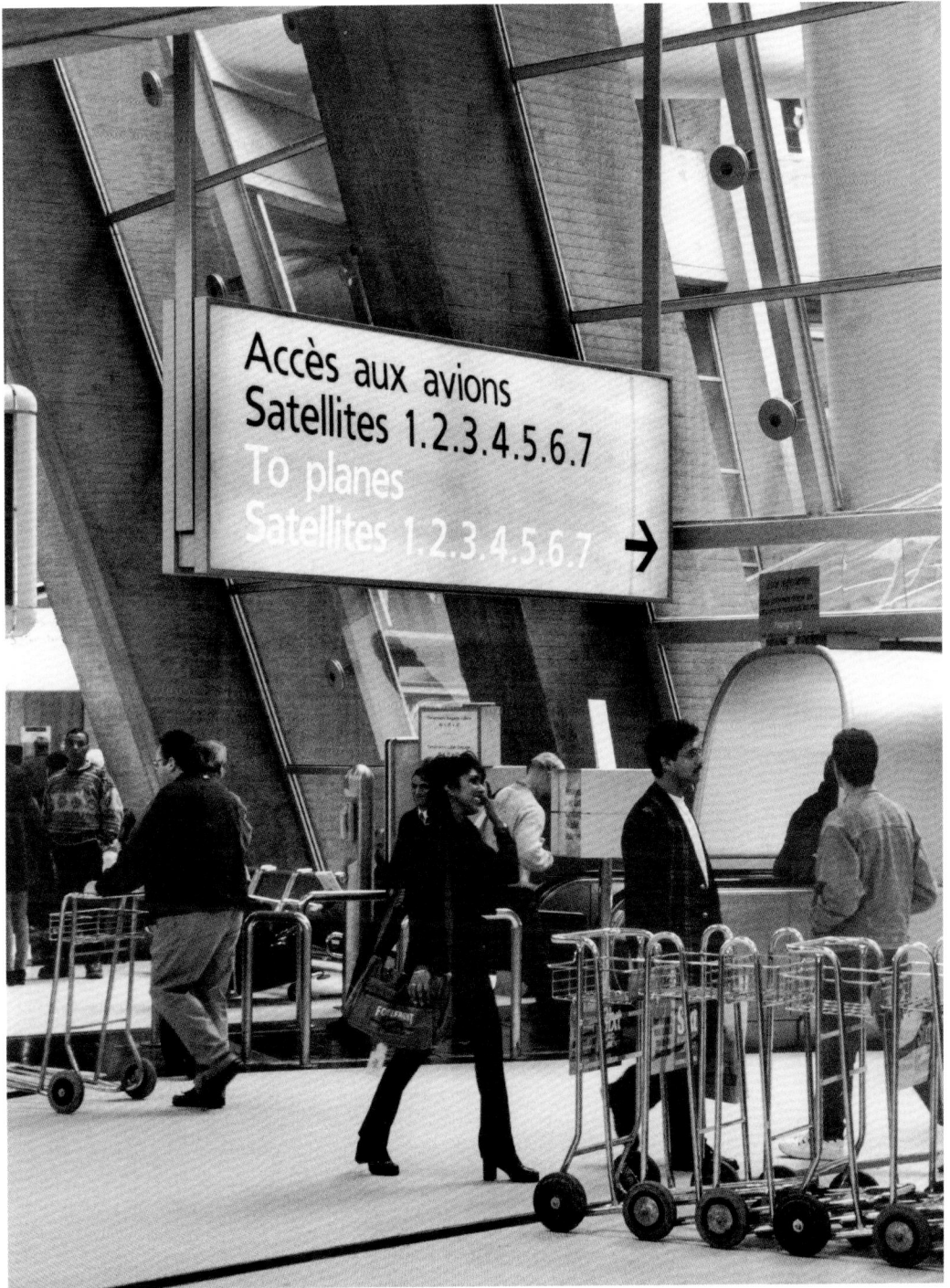

Accès aux avions
Satellites 1.2.3.4.5.6.7
To planes
Satellites 1.2.3.4.5.6.7 →

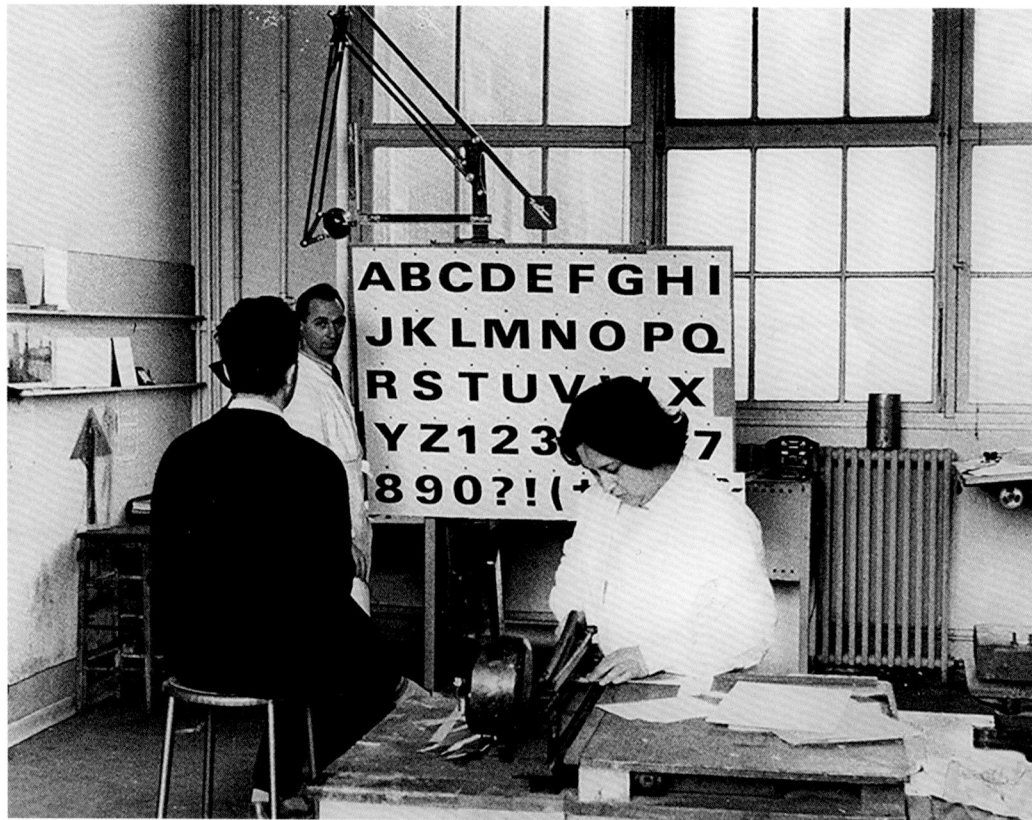

Frutiger overseeing the expansion of Univers at Deberny & Peignot in the 1950s.

The future is not Futura

In the early 1950s sans serif typefaces ruled, and Futura was considered the premier typeface in Europe; but Frutiger suggested to Charles Peignot, director of the Deberny & Peignot foundry, that he could design an alternative. Frutiger disliked geometric typefaces for being too rigid, so it's understandable that he wasn't a fan of Futura, even if that went against the prevailing opinion at the time (and full credit to Adrian, if you take on a giant, you go big or you go home).

Frutiger began sketches for a typeface called Le Monde (the World) in 1952. Like the principal designer of Helvetica and fellow Swiss native Max Miedinger, Frutiger took inspiration from Akzidenz-Grotesk. In so doing he inadvertently set up something of a rivalry between Univers and Helvetica, as they share a common ancestor.

When Frutiger showed Peignot the more developed designs for Le Monde, his boss could apparently barely contain his excitement, shouting, 'Good heavens, Adrian, that's the future!' (It's not recorded whether Peignot was generally known for his keen sense of irony.)

Peignot clearly felt Frutiger wasn't thinking on a grand enough scale with the working title of 'World'; although another contender was 'Galaxy', he insisted the name be changed to 'Universe' — in French, *Univers* — which became the final name when the typeface was released in 1957.

From the get-go, Univers offered a wide range of weights and widths. The original marketing materials referenced the periodic table, because the weights of Univers are named using numbers. The naming system makes Univers seem very scientific (and honestly just a little confusing), but it is not just a marketing gimmick, there is a purpose.

One of the frustrations of designing in Europe was that different languages had different terms for the same typographic elements. A bold font in German is *'fett'*, whereas in French it is *'gras'* and in Italian *'grassetto'* or *'negretto'*, leading to the possibility of mistranslation or misunderstandings.

In a system so elegant and practical as to distil the national character of Switzerland, the different faces were identified by numbers rather than names. Univers 55 meant the roman weight (5) in the normal width (5), Univers 56 meant the roman weight (5) set in italic (6), and so on. Typography meets an Excel spreadsheet before Microsoft had even been invented. (Although it must be admitted that inconsistencies have crept into usage over time.)

As well as delighting Frutiger's boss, Univers found a champion in Emil Ruder. The famous typography teacher from Basel enthusiastically promoted the new typeface in his magazine — with the catchy title of *Typographische Monatsblätter* — devoting all 12 covers in 1961 to showcasing the different weights and widths. Thanks to Peignot's friendship with John Dreyfus, the typographic advisor to the Monotype Corporation, Univers was a shoo-in for conversion for the Monotype machine in 1961.

It was beginning to look like Univers would become the new darling of European typography.

Original marketing material, designed by Adrian Frutiger, arranges Univers like a periodic table, and shows off the big font family with its wide range of weights.

21 variations sur un thème unique

univers

20 variantes
4 graisses
7 chasses
7 italiques

Debeny Peignot 18 rue Ferrus Paris Por 79-79

Pride comes before a fall

Sadly, around the same time it seems Frutiger made the fatal mistake of refusing Mike Parker permission to reduce the angle of the obliques in order to fit both the roman and italic characters on a single matrix.

Mike Parker was the director of typographic development at Mergenthaler Linotype, whose library of typefaces was on its way to becoming the industry standard. Univers was consequently not added to the Linotype library until 1969, by which time it had been overtaken, not necessarily by preference but through market saturation, by Helvetica.

We can appreciate the deep irony by which getting on his high horse brought Frutiger down. It's this decision that explains (at least in part) why there is a movie about Helvetica and not one about Univers.

Anatomy

Univers is a 'Lineal Neo-grotesque' typeface under the Vox type classification system. Neo-grotesques differ from Grotesques in that they have less stroke contrast and a more regular structure; however, that structure doesn't rigidly adhere to underlying squares, circles and triangles as in the Geometrics that Frutiger detested.

Some other defining characteristics are a low x-height, the rectangular tittle, and that the tail of the uppercase 'Q' runs along the baseline and not at an angle.

As previously noted, and like most Grotesques (or sans serifs), Univers features obliques rather than true italics. And when it comes to bang for your buck you really are spoiled for choice; when Univers was reissued as Linotype Univers it included a whopping 63 variants.

Univers   Futura

cap height
x-height
baseline

Univers in the wild

For anyone who likes their technology a little bit retro, prior to 2004 Apple Inc. used Univers Condensed Oblique (caps) on the keys of their Macintosh keyboards.

The typeface has been set in lowercase as the United Nations Children's Fund (UNICEF) logo since 2003. It was used in the branding for the 1972 (Munich) and 1976 (Montreal) Summer Olympics, and for the eBay logo. The FedEx logo combines Univers 67 with Futura (which Frutiger probably didn't like). The British Petroleum company's BP logo uses Univers 55, and the international money transfer corporation Western Union uses Univers Extra Black.

Kiss, date, marry or kill?

As demonstrated by the stable of corporates who have chosen Univers for their branding, this typeface has all the benefits of Helvetica, but with one distinct advantage: it isn't Helvetica. It doesn't come with all the baggage associated with being one of the most recognizable typefaces. You might say Helvetica has the flash, but Univers brings the muscle.

We're not sure either typeface is exactly marriage material, but dating Helvetica is akin to romancing a retired sports star or a soap actor — every time you went out together you'd be in danger of being elbowed aside for selfies with fans. Univers, on the other hand, seems like the sort of date that other people might look at twice, wondering where they'd seen it before, then leave you to be thoroughly entertained in the corner over a bottle of fine wine.

So maybe in his refusal to compromise, Adrian Frutiger did us all a favour.

Logos featuring Univers include UNICEF (above), FedEx (above right), Western Union (right) and the Munich Olympics (opposite).

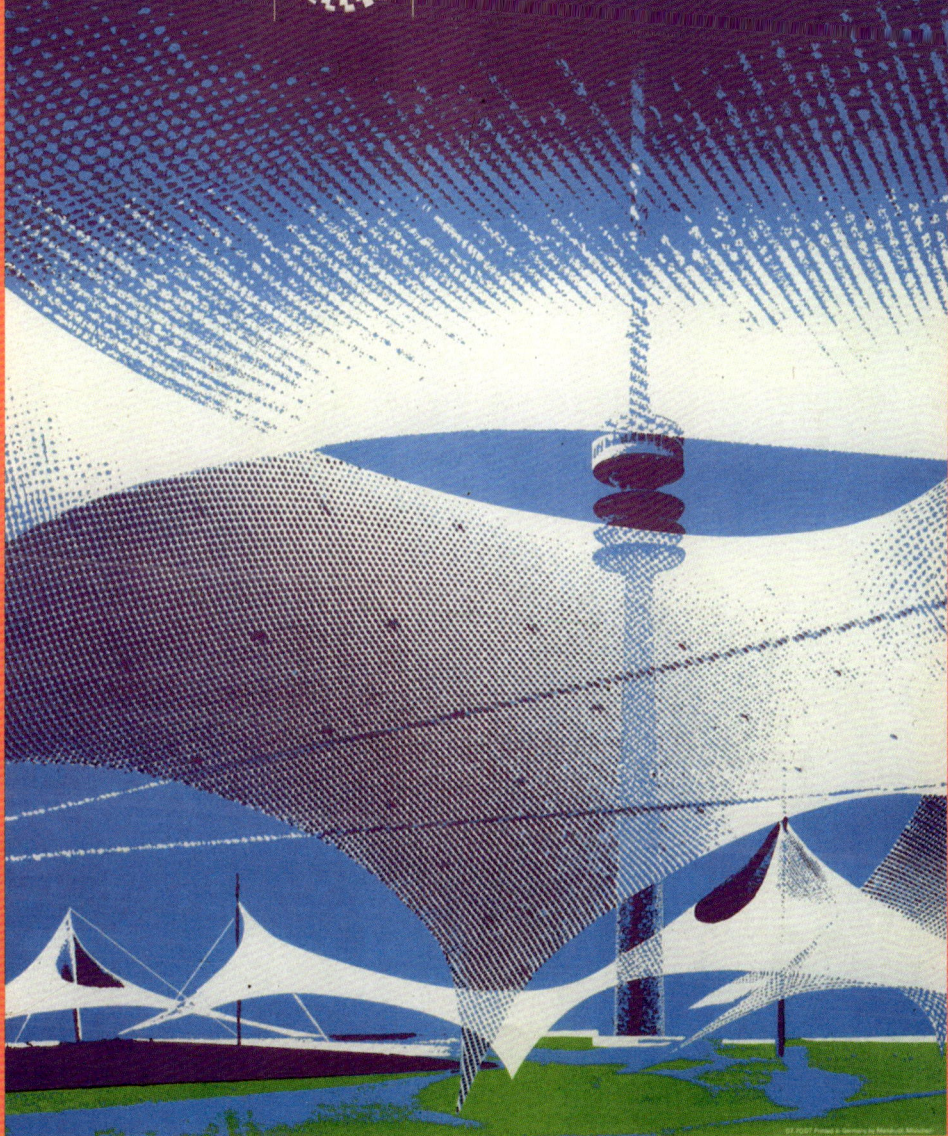

München  1972   26.8.–10.9.

Papyrus

Designer: Chris Costello
Date: 1982

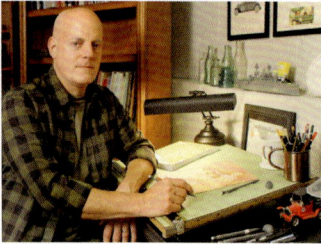

Portrait of Chris Costello.

There are two typefaces that are infamously linked to high type crimes and misdemeanours. One is Comic Sans, which we're not going to dignify with an entry in this book because, well, we have a professional reputation to maintain. The other is Papyrus — which even its creator agrees has been overused, and in ways for which it was never intended. Although, are there really any innocent victims in type crimes? We'll let you decide.

The boy who drew

Chris Costello was born in Kingston, New York, and grew up in the 1960s and 70s — a time of flower power, free love and magic mushrooms, when people who should have known better ignored the guard-rails of social niceties (and, some would argue, good taste). Let's face it, the story of Papyrus is the story of people who should have known better.

Costello's father was a graphic artist and sign painter, and Costello attributes his interest in design, but specifically typography, to helping his dad paint signs and illustrate brochures while still in elementary school. This led him first to a community college degree in commercial art, then to enrolment at the Art Institute of Fort Lauderdale, Florida — a choice Costello admits was made primarily based on its location adjacent to the beach.

Intending to take only one semester off from studying, Costello secured employment as an entry-level designer and illustrator for an advertising agency in South Florida. There could be significant downtime between projects, so he occupied himself by doodling and drawing his own illustrations and lettering. Honestly, who among us has not been guilty of a little light doodling during work time? One attempt to stave off boredom evolved into the typeface Papyrus: just one more thing the advertising industry should answer for.

abcdefghijklm
nopqrstuvwxyz
ABCDEFGHIJKLM
NOPQRSTUVWXYZ
0123456789!?

abcdefghijklm
nopqrstuvwxyz
ABCDEFGHIJKLM
NOPQRSTUVWXYZ
0123456789!?

After a year, Costello parlayed the full-time position into the more lucrative field of freelance work. He moved to Boston, Massachusetts, to work as an advertising agency art director, before again dividing his time between freelance illustration and design and touring as a professional bass guitarist.

He continued to work in publishing and marketing, both in-house and as a freelancer, with an impressive clientele list that included Simon & Schuster, Random House, Oxford University Press, Little, Brown and Company, and HarperCollins. In 2003 Costello finally completed his long-delayed bachelors degree from Northeastern University, Boston. As of 2016, he was designing coinage for the US mint.

Costello designed several typefaces, notably Mirage and Blackstone, but none has acquired the notoriety of Papyrus.

(above right) Sheet of Papyrus script.
(right and opposite) Some of Costello's sketches of Papyrus.

Killing time

Papyrus was created in 1982 when Costello was 23 and — as we've established — bored at work and apparently thinking about the Bible. (We're not saying those things automatically go together; draw your own conclusions.) He toyed with the idea of what English-language texts would look like if written on papyrus 2000 years ago, an effect he achieved with a calligraphy pen and textured paper. Over the course of four days, he designed a complete uppercase character set: it had been a slow three months in the office.

Of the 10 type foundries that Costello submitted his design to, Letraset was the only one who showed an interest. However, they insisted on both an upper- and lowercase set of characters, and they wanted the letter strokes to be thicker. Little wonder, given the general experience with Letraset. The Letraset designers were probably already consigning Chris Costello to a special place in hell. Costello spent the next several months of his spare time creating 10cm- (4in-) tall masters of his letterforms, sometimes after working up as many as 30 examples of each character to establish a unified set. Letraset purchased the typeface from him for US$750 (the equivalent today of around $2400).

A whimper not a bang

After all that hard work, when Papyrus first appeared in the Letraset catalogue in 1984 it was pretty much ignored. In fact, it languished in the popularity stakes for more than a decade, until Letraset licensed its fonts for desktop publishing in the mid-1990s. Papyrus was chosen by Microsoft type director Robert Norton to extend the design breadth of Microsoft Publisher, and pre-installed as part of Microsoft Office 97. (Famously tasteful Apple didn't include Papyrus as part of the Mac OS suitcase until 2003.)

It's estimated that because Papyrus is installed by default, one in seven people on planet Earth have access to this typeface. That's at least one billion people (and yes, Costello regrets signing the rights over).

Examining the body

In the Vox type classification system, 'Calligraphics' is a broad and somewhat odds-and-ends category, including typefaces that defy easy description. Papyrus sits within the 'Scripts' subcategory, as it imitates penmanship. The identifying characteristic of this typeface is the notched, rough edges to the strokes.

In fairness to Costello and as difficult as it may be for us to admit, by many standards Papyrus is a well-constructed typeface. It features wide characters, large counterforms, and long ascenders and descenders in proportion to the x-height, all of which contribute to an even grey (the ideal) when set in a block of text.

The letterforms are constructed from modulated strokes, and these are largely consistent across the typeface, with matching curves in the lowercase 'c' and 'd', and 'e' and 'o'. Similarly, the shoulders of the 'n', 'm' and 'h' complement each other. The same cannot be said of the characters in Comic Sans, for instance, which are irregular and therefore don't sit evenly, causing issues with kerning.

Some of the original promotional materials for Papyrus.

Costello lists William Morris and other Arts & Crafts artists among his influences, and there is something evocative of Charles Rennie Mackintosh's Willow Tea Rooms signage in the proportions of the uppercase letters.

One of the criticisms levelled at Papyrus, unfairly perhaps but accurately, is that it is a fantasy. A fake. We're not suggesting that Costello perpetrated a hoax on an unsuspecting design community — to the best of our knowledge he's been nothing but honest about the origins of his typeface. But in refining and regulating his letterforms over weeks and months using modern technologies and a 20th-century aesthetic, they are very far removed from the rough transcriptions on actual papyrus that have survived from antiquity. This is an example of what has been referred to as 'material dishonesty' — in the same way that a faux marble tile in your bathroom has very little in common with a quarry in Carrara.

Although these fantasies might seem innocent, they can perpetuate unhelpful tropes, especially through the nexus of New Age and ancient or Indigenous cultures, for which Papyrus has become something of a catch-all. Which brings us to…

Lorem ipsum

d o m h

comparison of curves and shoulders

often   often

Papyrus   *Comic Sans*

BREAKFAST MENU

Willow Tea Rooms branding based on letters designed by Mackintosh

Papyrus in the wild

Where to begin? Despite its presence on countless computers worldwide, Costello receives a negligible, if ongoing, royalty payment for his typeface (which perhaps should be investigated as the proceeds of crime… Because, make no mistake about it, once everyone was armed with Papyrus, a typographic crime spree had begun).

Since 2008 a website named Papyrus Watch has been logging Papyrus sightings. It currently resides on the X social media platform.

We must mention the 2018 *Saturday Night Live* sketch starring Ryan Gosling. Like all great satire, although the subject is one thing (Papyrus), the target is something different — in this case skewering both the digital design process and the Hollywood blockbuster machine represented by the film franchise *Avatar*.

Ironically (and albeit before Costello worked for them), the US Mint experienced technical difficulties with Papyrus when they used it for the lettering on a series of Congressional Gold Medals issued in 2008. The notches and nicks defeated their high-tech mould-carving equipment, so they banned it from future designs.

Kiss, date, marry or kill?

Arguably the worst villains exist in fiction, and the worst of the worst exist in comic books, making Papyrus the Harley Quinn to Comic Sans's Joker — neither of which anyone would want to associate with. As Batman can attest, some villains just won't seem to die.

So, yes, we'd opt to kill. But if that seems harsh, let's give the last word to another classic animated character, Jessica Rabbit, who, in the movie *Who Framed Roger Rabbit?* delivered the famous line: 'I'm not bad, I'm just drawn that way.'

If you've read this far and are still determined to use Papyrus, don't say we didn't warn you.

(right and bottom right) Ryan Gosling spoke for us all in his takedown of the producers of *Avatar*; it seems to have shamed James Cameron into adjusting the typeface for the *Avatar* sequels.

(below) Perhaps the worst (or maybe the best?) use is a talking skeleton in the video game *Undertale*, who exclusively talks in pop-up speech bubbles set in Papyrus.

(bottom) Your authors in front of a restaurant we chose because it is the only correct use of Papyrus we have ever seen (the food was excellent too).

(opposite) Papyrus can mean many things to many people, from selling groceries to alternative medicine.

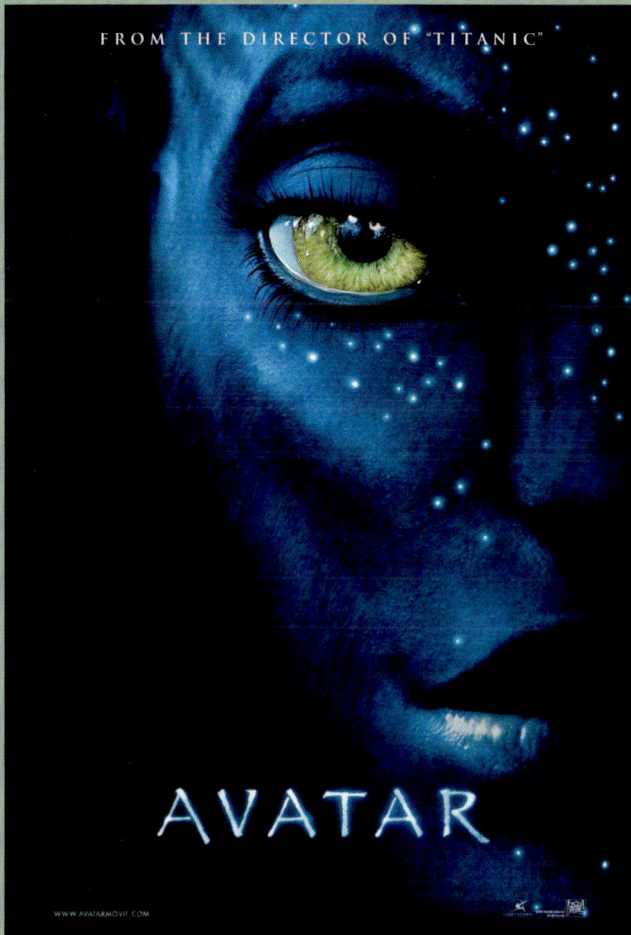

FURTHER READING

Here are some of the most interesting and useful books, articles and websites that we used to research this book. Enjoy.

Books

Blackwell, Lewis, *Twentieth Century Type* (London: Laurence King, 2004)

Bringhurst, Robert, *The Elements of Typographic Style*, 4th edition (Seattle, WA: Hartley & Marks, 2019)

Burke, Christopher, *Paul Renner* (New York: Princeton Architectural Press, 1999)

Busic-Snyder, Cynthia, and Kate Clair, *A Typographic Workbook: a primer to history, techniques, and artistry*, 3rd edition (New York: Wiley, 2008)

Garfield, Simon, *Just My Type* (London: Profile Books, 2011)

Haslam, Andrew, *Lettering: a reference manual of techniques* (London: Laurence King, 2011)

Lupton, Ellen, *Thinking with Type*, 3rd edition (New York: Princeton Architectural Press, 2024)

Macmillan, Neil, *An A–Z of Type Designers*, (London: Laurence King, 2006)

McCarthy, Fiona, *Eric Gill* (London: Faber & Faber, 2020). (We don't recommend you look for the original diary extracts, you won't be able to unread them.)

Meggs, Philip B., and Alston W. Purvis, *Meggs History of Graphic Design*, 6th edition (New York: Wiley, 2016)

Meggs, Philip B., Ben Day, Sandra Maxa, Rob Carter and Mark Sanders, *Typographic Design: form and communication*, 7th edition (New York: Wiley, 2018)

Morison, Stanley, *A Tally of Types*, revised edition (Cambridge: Cambridge University Press, 1973)

Stock-Allen, Nancy, *Carol Twombly: her brief but brilliant career in type design* (New Castle, Delaware: Oak Knoll Press, 2016)

Tschichold, Jan, *The Form of the Book: essays on the morality of good design* (London: Lund Humphries Publishers Ltd, 1992)

Zapf, Hermann, *Alphabet Stories: a chronicle of technical developments* (Rochester, NY: RIT Cary Graphic Arts Press, 2008)

Websites and articles in chapter order:

Introduction

The International Type Association, ATypI: atypi.org/

Everything you ever wanted to know about the Linotype machine, from the Library of Congress: blogs.loc.gov/headlinesandheroes/2022/06/the-linotype-the-machine-that-revolutionized-movable-type/

Times New Roman

Essay about Times New Roman by Stanley Morison, published in *Eye Magazine*. It goes deep on the typographic design of the typeface – very deep: www.eyemagazine.com/feature/article/stanley-morison-changing-the-times

Fascinating video about the last day of hot metal typesetting at the *New York Times* in the short film *Farewell* (1978): https://vimeo.com/127605643

The website Typography for Lawyers has great information about type and is not just for lawyers; we share the same view of Times New Roman: https://typographyforlawyers.com/a-brief-history-of-times-new-roman.html

Gill Sans

Thoughtful essay on Eric Gill and Catholicism, published in 2017, about the opening of the controversial exhibition 'Eric Gill: the body' at the Ditchling Museum of Art and Craft: www.apollo-magazine.com/eric-gills-fall-from-grace/

Bodoni

Hey – why don't you visit the Bodoni Museum in Parma? https://museobodoniano.com/

This is the best Australian chicken parma recipe that we know of – enjoy: www.recipetineats.com/chicken-parmigiana/

Goudy

The Library of Congress has a special archive of Fred and Bertha Goudy's work (you know, if you like that kind of thing): https://guides.loc.gov/frederic-and-bertha-goudy-collection

An explanation of the Errol Morris study of readers in the *New York Times*: www.fastcompany.com/1670556/are-some-fonts-more-believable-than-others

Baskerville
A scholarly account of how often John Baskerville's coffin was opened: www.tandfonline.com/doi/full/10.1080/0047729X.2022.2126238#abstract

Akzidenz-Grotesk
The detailed history of Akzidenz-Grotesk that convinced us about its origins: https://klim.co.nz/blog/new-details-about-origins-akzidenz-grotesk/

The secret history of women in industrial type: www.women-in-type.com/

A lecture about the project explaining Type Drawing Offices, given by Alice Savoie in 2020: https://vimeo.com/460376476

Mrs Eaves
Famous 'The cult of the ugly', essay by Steven Heller, written at the height of the 'legibility wars': www.eyemagazine.com/feature/article/cult-of-the-ugly And Steven Heller's reassessment mea culpa article for *Print* magazine in 2016: https://docslib.org/doc/781816/revisiting-the-so-called-legibility-wars-of-the-80s-and

Why don't you buy yourself a copy of *Emigre* magazine? www.emigre.com/Magazine

Trajan
Article about the Trajan rubbing by Edward Catich from the rather wonderful Letterform Archive: https://letterformarchive.org/news/this-just-in-trajan-rubbing-and-recutting/

Novarese
We are still waiting for our invitation to Les Rencontres de Lure www.delure.org/en

Read about the Les Rencontres de Lure gathering, and Maximilien Vox, here: www.grapheine.com/en/graphic-design-en/secrets-rencontres-de-lure

Bell Centennial
This 2011 interview with Matthew Carter in *Print* magazine illustrates his extraordinary career: www.printmag.com/designer-interviews/an-interview-with-matthew-carter/

'Speak Up' blog article from 2008, from the UnderConsideration archives, about the Bell Centennial monograph published by AT&T in 1982: www.underconsideration.com/speakup/archives/005274.html

Foundry Sterling
Wonderful interview with Freda Sack about Letraset by Adrian Shaughnessy: https://uniteditions.com/blogs/news/letraset-interview-freda-sack

An interview with Freda Sack, where she describes the working process at The Foundry: www.thefoundrytypes.com/codex-3-the-journal-of-letterforms-summer-2013-part-3-of-3/

David Quay and Stuart de Rozario's account of the design process of Foundry Sterling: www.typeroom.eu/the-foundry-types-david-quay-on-the-rebirth-of-an-iconic-type-design-affair

It's not just our opinion – Letraset sucks: https://hullabaloo.co.uk/blog/whatever-happened-letraset/

This obituary is one of many that describes what a lovely human Freda Sack was: www.alphabettes.org/freda-sack-1951-2019/

Transport
The Jock Kinneir Library has a great collection of his work with Margaret Calvert: https://jockkinneirlibrary.org/

If you are in the UK, you can watch Margaret Calvert help James May deface a Men at Work sign in episode 7 of series 14 of *Top Gear* on BBC iPlayer: www.bbc.co.uk/iplayer/episode/b00pws33/top-gear-series-14-episode-7

Zapf Dingbats
Comprehensive obituary of Hermann, 'Why we (heart) Zapf Dingbats' https://amp.theguardian.com/artanddesign/shortcuts/2015/jun/10/why-we-love-hermann-zapf

Everything you ever wanted to know about emojis: www.smithsonianmag.com/science-nature/the-accidental-history-of-the-symbol-18054936/

Univers
Good work into mental health research continues at the Adrian and Simone Frutiger foundation, which uses Univers in its branding (of course): www.fondationfrutiger.ch/de/stiftung

Papyrus
Chris Costello ignores the cringe and talks about his greatest work, Papyrus: https://chriscostello.design/fonts/

INDEX

Back to Font

PICTURE CREDITS

p8 Zoonar GmbH/Alamy Stock Photo; p9t © Daniel Pype; p9c History and Art Collection/Alamy Stock Photo; p9b The History Collection/Alamy Stock Photo; p11 Photo by Jessica Fiess-Hill https://commons.wikimedia.org/wiki/File:French_Clarendon_wood_type.jpg; p12 EMU history/Alamy Stock Photo; p13 © Chetham's Library/Bridgeman Images; p14 From the British Library archive/Bridgeman Images; p18 Chronicle/Alamy Stock Photo; p20 The Times/News Licensing, photo: John Frost Newspapers; p22t Courtesy of the authors; p22b Photo by Petri Aukia https://commons.wikimedia.org/w/index.php?curid=46682029; p23t © Science Photo Library; p24 Courtesy of the authors; p26 Courtesy of the authors; p27 AJ Pics/Alamy Stock Photo; p28 Pictorial Press Ltd/Alamy Stock Photo; p30t St Bride Library; p30b © Alex Ramsay; p31 Photo by David Castor https://commons.wikimedia.org/wiki/File:Prospero_and_Ariel-1.jpg; p32 Photo by Andy Scott https://commons.wikimedia.org/wiki/File:Westminster_Cathedral,_Stations_of_the_Cross_XIV.jpg; p34t Artepics/Alamy Stock Photo; p34b Courtesy of the authors; p35t Photo by Bruno Martins on Unsplash; p35b Fox Photos/Getty Images; p38tl Photo by K.Mitch Hodge on Unsplash; p38bl Photo by Siora Photography on Unsplash; p38r Steven May/Alamy Stock Photo; p39 Photo by Heidi Fin on Unsplash; p40 Andrea Haushofer Archive, Munich (© photo E. Wasow); p42 Klingspor Museum, Offenbach am Main; p43 Album/Alamy Stock Photo; p44b Photo by Jakayla Toney on Unsplash; p45 Andrea Haushofer Archive, Munich; p46 Klingspor Museum, Offenbach am Main; p47b © Stadtarchiv München, Signatur: DE-1992-BUR-0453-002; p50t Photo by Adam Kolmacka on Unsplash; p50bl Photo by Carlos Macías on Unsplash; p50br Photo by Vishu Joo on Unsplash; p51tl Photo by Omar Abascal on Unsplash; p51tr FlixPix/Alamy Stock Photo; p51br Courtesy of the Missouri State Archives, MS192 Gerald Massie Photograph Collection; p52 VTR/Alamy Stock Photo; p54 Stefano Bianchetti/Bridgeman Images; p55 Edoardo Fornaciari/Getty Images; p57 Photo by Toa Heftiba on Unsplash; p58l Jeremy Moeller/Getty Images; p58r Associated Press/Alamy Stock Photo; p59t Photo by Mathias Reding on Unsplash; p59bl Dan Wilton/PYMCA/Avalon/Getty Images; p59br Eric Carr/Alamy Stock Photo; p60 Genthe photograph collection, Library of Congress, Prints and Photographs Division; p62t Courtesy of the authors; p62b Frederic W. Goudy Collection, Library of Congress, Rare Book and Special Collections Division; p63 Courtesy of the authors; p66 Courtesy of the authors; p67t JHVEPhoto/Shutterstock.com; p67cl BFA/Alamy Stock Photo; p67cr Courtesy of the authors; p67b Valeriya Zankovych/Alamy Stock Photo; p68 Historical image collection by Bildagentur-online/Alamy Stock Photo; p70 Beinecke Rare Book and Manuscript Library; p71l piemags/RTM/Alamy Stock Photo; p71r Courtesy Museum of Printing, Massachusetts; p72t Courtesy Tim Bryars; p72b Courtesy of the authors; p74l Beinecke Rare Book and Manuscript Library; p74r Peter Harrington, 2024; p75 Reproduced with permission of the Library of Birmingham, Pershouse collection of Birmingham illustrations Vol II (MS 897); p77t Michael Nagle/Bloomberg via Getty Images; p77b Andriy Blokhin/Shutterstock.com; p78 CC0 @ Stiftung Deutsches Technikmuseum Berlin; p80 From the collection of Letterform Archive; p82t From Hermann Hoffmann Das Haus Berthold (1921), photo courtesy of Dan Reynolds; p82b Archiv für Buchdruckerkunst, 1896 https://en.m.wikipedia.org/wiki/File:Schattierte_Grotesk_1896_(cropped).jpg; p83t & b © Monotype archives; p84l © Monotype archives; p84r Stiftung Deutsches Technikmuseum Berlin, Historisches Archiv, VI.1.037 042-011; p85 From a brochure in the Monotype archives; p87tl Photo by PCHS-NJROTC https://commons.wikimedia.org/wiki/File:American_Red_Cross_in_El_Jobean.jpg; p87bl Creative Commons; p87r Sander Koning/EPA/Shutterstock; p88 Courtesy of Emigre; p90 Courtesy of Emigre; p92l & r Courtesy of Emigre; p93t Penta Springs Limited/Alamy Stock Photo; p93b Beinecke Rare Book and Manuscript Library; p94l & r Courtesy of Emigre; p96 Courtesy Claire Mason; p97t Francis Vachon/Alamy Stock Photo; p97b Courtesy Nono Ampuy and Martin Lavielle; p98 © Dennis Hearne; p100 Alinari/TopFoto; p101 St. Ambrose University Archives; p102 Fela Sanu/Shutterstock.com; p103 Courtesy of the authors; p105l © Universal/Courtesy Everett Collection/Mary Evans; p105tc Album/Alamy Stock Photo; p105tr Photo 12/Alamy Stock Photo; p105cl AJ Pics/Alamy Stock Photo; p105cr Maximum Film/Alamy Stock Photo; p105b Ken Howard/Alamy Stock Photo; p106 Tipoteca Italiana Fondazione, Cornuda (Treviso), Italy; p108t Tipoteca Italiana Fondazione, Cornuda (Treviso), Italy; p108b From the collection of Letterform Archive; p109t Pvstockmedia/shutterstock.com; p109b Tipoteca Italiana Fondazione, Cornuda (Treviso), Italy; p110t & b Tipoteca Italiana Fondazione, Cornuda (Treviso), Italy; p113tl Lubo Ivanko/Shutterstock.com; p113tr EyeBrowz/Alamy Stock Photo; p113b Oleksandr Prykhodko/Alamy Stock Photo; p114t Photo Courtesy John D. and Catherine T. MacArthur Foundation; p114b Maximum Film/Alamy Stock Photo; p116t © Private Eye; p116b Michael Vi/shutterstock.com; p119t gvictoria/shutterstock.com; p119b Courtesy Armin Vit; p121t & b Courtesy Armin Vit; p122 Courtesy Armin Vit; p123 Courtesy Armin Vit; p124 © Jason Wen; p126 Ian Goodrick/Alamy Stock Photo; p127 Photography by Catherine Dixon and Phil Baines; p129t Mick Sinclair/Alamy Stock Photo; p129b Photo by Reisetopia on Unsplash; p130 Neil Spence/Alamy Stock Photo; p132t Courtesy Margaret Calvert; p132b © Jock Kinneir Library; p133l & r BBCMG via Gettyimages; p134 urbanbuzz/Alamy Stock Photo; p135 Peter Andrew Richardson/Alamy Stock Photo; p136t & b St Bride Library;

ACKNOWLEDGEMENTS

p137 The National Archives; p138 Kristoffer Tripplaar/ Alamy Stock Photo; p139t melissamn/Shutterstock.com; p139b Memories Over Mocha/Shutterstock.com; p140 Rochester Institute of Technology Archives, Rochester, NY; p144t & c Herzog August Bibliothe04 Wolfenbüttel; p144b John Bracegirdle/Alamy Stock Photo; p145 Sophie James/ Shutterstock.com; p149bl Courtesy VASAVA ARTWORKS S.L., Barcelona, Client: ICEX España Exportación e Inversiónes, Artwork: Vasava Studio; p149br Courtesy of the authors; p150 KEYSTONE/Ayse Yavas; p152 Courtesy of the Museum für Gestaltung Zürich, Graphics Collection, ZHdK; p153 Courtesy of the Museum für Gestaltung Zürich, Graphics Collection, ZHdK; p154 Russ Bishop/Alamy Stock Photo; p155 Courtesy of the Museum für Gestaltung Zürich, Graphics Collection, ZHdK; p156 Courtesy of the Museum für Gestaltung Zürich, Graphics Collection, ZHdK; p157t Lettering, Printing and Graphic Design Collection at the University of Reading; p157b Courtesy of the Museum für Gestaltung Zürich, Graphics Collection, ZHdK; p160tl ricochet64/Shutterstock.com; p160tr TMP - An Instant of Time/Shutterstock.com; p160b Donald Trung Quoc Don https://commons.wikimedia.org/wiki/File:Western_Union_ Schiedamseweg,_Delfshaven,_Rotterdam_(2023)_02.jpg; p161 Retro AdArchives/Alamy Stock Photo; p162 © Anita Costello; p164t & b © Chris Costello; p165 © Chris Costello; p166 © Chris Costello; p168l & r Courtesy of the authors; p169tl Courtesy of Undertale; p169tr BFA/Alamy Stock Photo; p169bl Courtesy of the authors; p169br Lauren Clements/NBC via Getty Images

To our loyal podcast listeners, we hope you enjoy this book; and if you are unfamiliar with *The Type Pod*, we invite you to check it out wherever you get your podcasts.

To Inger, our producer, who works tirelessly (and sometimes fruitlessly) to rein in our worst impulses on air, this book expresses your voice too – thank you. We literally couldn't have done this without you. Likewise to the people who taught us about type, especially Steve, Mary and Tony: thanks for making us into the giant type nerds we are today.

To all the team at Laurence King: Liz, for her unflagging enthusiasm, support and insight; Gaynor, for her rigorous fact-checking and input; Sophie, who rose to every image permissions challenge (and there were many!); and Roger, who weathered the demands of two book designers who chose not to design their own book. Thank you.

To our families and friends (even the ones who don't listen to the pod), thank you for your constant encouragement, interest and devotion.

And to Thor the cat, who helped get the ball rolling.